Praise for *The Other Classroom*

"Michael Coffino reminds us of both the tremendous opportunity and great responsibility all who work in high school athletics have to our students. He provides concrete examples of ways to enhance the experience for all in achieving the desire outcomes. It is a must read."—**Bob Gardner, executive director, National Federation of State High School Associations**

"Michael Coffino is spot on in his description of the specific qualities and characteristics a good coach can draw out of the high school athlete. Every high school athletic director and administrator needs to read *The Other Classroom* to 1) be reminded of the importance of prep sports; and 2) to fully understand the range of qualifications a potential high school coach must have to properly guide his/her players to their full potential." The importance of high school athletics to a developing and maturing adolescent can never be undervalued."—**Tony Dorado, Nike's National Manager of High School Basketball**

"Coach Coffino has crafted an essential handbook for how high school coaches and athletic administrators can and should create the best learning environments for the adolescents under their charge, so they may flourish at that crucial stage of their development. As *The Other Classroom* so powerfully shows, high school coaches occupy a special place as guardians: a calling to help our youth become good people first and good athletes second."—**Timothy Holley, director of athletics, Gilman School**

"A wonderful read for anyone who has ever played, cheered, watched or coached high school sports. Essential reading for parents of kids who are involved in, or will one day play, high school sports. When the trophies, plaques and banners are all collecting dust, Coffino's teachings and observations will be in the heart and mind of every former high school athlete turned college graduate, professional, parent and mentor. Excellent book."—**Rich Cellini, professor, sport management program, University of San Francisco**

"*The Other Classroom* is essential reading for all high school administrators, principals, faculty, athletic directors, coaches, and parents. Mr. Coffino's book is a profoundly thoughtful, research and evidence based, study on the extensive scope of positive effects resulting from truly integrated academic and sport high school curricula. He persuasively details the great opportunities realized or lost in the development of the mind, psyche, and body, of our high school students."—**Leo Dorado, judge of the California Superior Court and former Division 1 (University of California, Berkeley) and professional European basketball player**

"Coach Coffino does an excellent job demonstrating that the high school arena is a vital extension of the classroom. His various illustrations and narrative pose challenges to every coach and athletic director to run impactful athletic programs and help our athletes become the next leaders in our society."—**Timothy Johnston, certified athletic administrator and director of athletics, East Grand Rapids High School**

"Michael Coffino makes a clear case for the value of high school athletics. While there are many critics who question the role of athletics in schools, Michael shows how transformational high school sports can be. It is not just an extracurricular activity but rather a very important part of the educational process. This book should be read by administrators, coaches, parents and athletes. When parents and athletes feel that travel teams are more important than high school athletics this book might help them think otherwise."—**Steve Young, CMAA, director of athletics, New Rochelle High School**

"*The Other Classroom* demonstrates that value-driven high school athletic programs help develop attributes, like integrity, leadership, confidence and self-esteem, that become lifelong character traits, as well as valuable skills that enhance academic performance and future careers. A highly recommended resource for anyone interested in education or athletics."—**Jennifer Turpin, professor of sociology, former provost and academic vice president, University of San Francisco**

"Michael Coffino makes a provocative case that the skills learned playing high school sports can be more important than English or chemistry to success in later life."—**Clara Hemphill, Pulitzer Prize–winning journalist and recognized expert on New York City public schools**

"Michael Coffino's *The Other Classroom* is a timely statement on a topic consuming millions of adults and youths across our country. Among other essential contributions, Coffino shows how high school athletes have the potential for growth in conflict resolution, character, leadership, and citizenship. *The Other Classroom* speaks to the growing need to get high school sports right for our children and adults, for along with the potential for remarkable growth in sport participation comes the ever-growing negative consequence of failing to approach high school sports with an educator's perspective."—**John E. Tufte, Ed.D, author of *Crazy-Proofing High School Sports* and *The Wrong Emphasis: Kids Learn What Adults Teach***

"If you ever doubted the significant impact of high school athletics on the lives of our youth, read *The Other Classroom*. Michael Coffino does a magnificent job showing how high school athletics teach the principles, values and skills we hold dear as a nation, yet so often shun in academic offerings, including empathy, citizenship, leadership, teamwork and willingness to take calculated risk, critical traits for anyone entering the job market and having a productive life. It is essential reading for athletic directors, coaches, school administrators, parents and employers."—**Erin Lewellen, head women's basketball Coach, Emery High School, Emeryville, California**

The Other Classroom

The Other Classroom

The Essential Importance of High School Athletics

Michael J. Coffino

ROWMAN & LITTLEFIELD
Lanham • Boulder • New York • London

Published by Rowman & Littlefield
An imprint of The Rowman & Littlefield Publishing Group, Inc.
4501 Forbes Boulevard, Suite 200, Lanham, Maryland 20706
www.rowman.com

Unit A, Whitacre Mews, 26-34 Stannary Street, London SE11 4AB

British Library Cataloguing in Publication Information Available

Library of Congress Cataloging-in-Publication Data

Names: Coffino, Michael, author.
Title: The other classroom : the essential importance of high school
    athletics / Michael J. Coffino.
Description: Lanham : Rowman & Littlefield, [2018] | Includes bibliographical
    references and index.
Identifiers: LCCN 2018000354 (print) | LCCN 2018014616 (ebook) | ISBN
    9781538108079 (electronic) | ISBN 9781538108062 (hardcover : alk. paper) | ISBN
    9781538118672 (paperback)
Subjects: LCSH: School sports. | High school athletes—Education.
Classification: LCC GV346 (ebook) | LCC GV346 .C64 2018 (print) | DDC
    796.04/2—dc23
LC record available at https://lccn.loc.gov/2018000354

Printed in the United States of America

To all high school athletes—past, present, and future—
may your cup of promise fill to the brim
as you blaze trails to inspire us all.

Contents

Acknowledgments

A heartfelt and deep expression of gratitude goes to each of the many people who spent their time sharing their athletic and life experiences, as well as their genuine enthusiasm for the subject matter of this book, including Coach Aidan Coffino, Alan Cotler, Alyson Lao, Andrew Klein, Bill Lefkowitz, Coach Bill Washauer, Bobby Savulich, Brett Cutler, Coco Lefkowitz, Coach Doug Young, Coach Eliot Smith, Gabriel Stricker, Coach Gini Ullery, Hossain Albgal, Jared Pickard, Jason Pickard, Jason Winship, Jimmy Sopko, Coach Jon Black, Professor Kevin Kniffin, LaRon Bullock, Coach Marianne Reilly, Coach Michael Bobino, Coach Michael Evans, Nicole Siminoff, Coach Patricia Dougherty, Patrick Ebke, Rebecca Watson, Sara Olson, Coach Torin Coffino, and Coach Stephanie Gaitley.

Thanks to the countless athletes I had the privilege to coach, even if we didn't always see eye to eye or I befuddled you with game decisions and strategies. We worked hard together, and you inspired me each step of the way. I will be forever grateful for the opportunity to coach and teach you.

Thank you, a second time, my sons and coaches, Torin Coffino and Aidan Coffino, for your support and characteristically insightful input on manuscript content.

I also must acknowledge again the coach standard-bearer, the inestimable Coach Eliot Smith, my first coaching mentor. Your contributions to the development and well-being of athletes, both youth and high school, and your timeless inspiration of your coaching colleagues, deserve special and repeated recognition, and a huge expression of gratitude. You are a model for coaches for all time.

A tip of the hat and a deep bow to the late Dan Buckley of La Salle Academy, old school for sure but a person of character and values first, and coach of the great game of basketball second, always a class act.

xii   *Acknowledgments*

Thank you Robert Stricker for your continued, ever-accessible counsel and for being my sounding board throughout my writing career.

Thank you Sharon Brusman for your reliable, timely, and quality transcriptions.

Much thanks to Loretta and David Stotter for your unconditional willingness to help me find wonderfully suited people to interview and enthusiastic support of this project.

Thank you Christen Karniski, once again, for believing in yet another of my projects.

And, not least, thanks to my sweet partner and muse, the incomparable Nancy Pickard, whose selfless support and candid input were indispensable and refreshing, and who graces my every day by dint of her core character.

Preface

Sports is human life in microcosm.

—Howard Cosell[1]

*F*rankly, it hadn't occurred to me that the high school where I was varsity basketball head coach hadn't invited me to the upcoming graduation ceremony. I knew next to nothing about high school graduation protocol, and the event wasn't on my radar. Besides, once the basketball season ended in March, other than intermittent attention to scheduling games for the next season and outlining the summer basketball program, my attention had turned primarily to "day job." As graduation edged closer, however, a few of my senior players formally invited me to attend graduation, cashing in on their few allocated graduation guest invitations. I came to learn that only the school's classroom teaching faculty received automatic invitations to graduation, to the exclusion of a narrowly defined group of coaches who were not salaried academic staff. For anyone in the excluded group to attend, a senior had to cough up a precious guest invitation.

The characteristic that denied certain coaches automatic graduation invitations was our status as "off-campus" or, less charitably described, "walk-on" coaches, which meant we did not teach in a traditional classroom—that familiar space set up with a blackboard, pieces of chalk, a desk, and rows of chairs. The graduation invitations the school extended as a matter of course to *other* head coaches had nothing to do with their roles as coaches and everything to do with their separate status as faculty operating in the traditional classroom, for example, an English teacher who happened to coach cross-country. The bottom line, in this context at least, was that the school didn't sufficiently value the contributions we head coaches made every year to merit inclusion in the crowning celebratory event of the school year, where graduating seniors were ushered into the next phase of their lives armed with boundless potential.

The exclusion seemed uninformed and wrong—no small irony for an educational institution. I knew well the durable impact high school coaches, "off" and "on" campus, have on the lives of student-athletes, in ways, I believed, more profound and pervasive than what students experience in traditional classrooms. The systemic exclusion from graduation of significant contributors to the well-being and future of students was more than a personal slight and failure to honor certain coaches; it struck me as a flaw in institutional values.

More recently, as discussed in chapter 1, certain commentary began to creep into the national media criticizing high school athletics and, in some more radical quarters, calling for their abolition. I carry no brief to argue that high school sports are free of blemish. For sure, most everyone with involvement in the high school experience knows of instances where high school athletics stubbed a toe or perhaps even went off the rails, for instance, a bully coach who badgered athletes or even struck an athlete, parents spewing invective from the stands, or, worse, attacking a game official, or adults who beat down their child's spirit because of unmet parental expectations or, more sordidly, supplied steroids to student-athletes. But a wholesale attack on this integral part of the high school experience seemed, to put it mildly, an attempt to throw the baby out with the bathwater and a fundamental failure to understand and honor the deep-rooted importance and enduring value of the high school athletic experience.

As a coach of many years with strong views about the short-term and long-term benefits of high school athletics, while the graduation slight irked me, the incipient cynicism about high school sports troubled me. In response, I wanted to do my small part to catapult the high school athletic experience to its rightful place in the *educational* pantheon, and this book became the vehicle.

The inextricable link between scholastic sports and the enduring well-being of our youth is inescapable.

Although I had ample experience and, of course, a set of views, to broaden my perspective, I conducted research and interviewed an array of former high school athletes, athletic directors, employers, and parents. The results were consistent with my decades of experience as a high school coach. High school athletics are not merely important additions to scholastic curricula. They are not, as commonly described, "extracurricular" or a mere "backdrop" to what else occurs on campus. They provide student-athletes unique experiences that give them tools to handle the varied challenges awaiting them after formal education and help empower them to find meaning and success in whatever they might do and become productive citizens. The inextricable link between scholastic sports and the enduring well-being of our youth is inescapable.

What follows is what I believe demonstrates the broad range and depth of the benefits—actual and potential—available to high school student-athletes. Perhaps someday, in turn, will follow invitations to all coaches to attend high school graduations.

Introduction

After coaching his team in the college football national championship, legendary coach Amos Alonzo Stagg was asked, "What do you think of your team?" He responded, "I'll let you know in 20 years."[1]

$\mathscr{A}$t their core, high school sports are an interactive immersion that uniquely prepares student-athletes for adult life and an ideal platform to prepare young women and men for what awaits them after they put away their school books. The lessons learned, tools acquired, and values instilled through a well-considered high school athletics program lay a robust foundation for student-athletes to enjoy advanced abilities to succeed on the life paths they travel after their formal education. As a transformative vehicle, high school sports function as a powerful rite of passage from adolescence to adulthood unlike any other in our culture.

I will go further. In terms of preparing youth for adult life, the high school athletic experience is a superior vehicle to any traditional classroom activity or course curriculum. While to a limited extent the athletic and academic experiences can touch on similar skills, in the main, what occurs in a vigorous and inspired high school athletic program has substantially greater reach and more profound and enduring impact than anything a traditional high school classroom can offer.

$\mathscr{I}$n terms of preparing youth for adult life, the high school athletic experience is a superior vehicle to any traditional classroom activity or course curriculum.

While high school athletic programs have differences, they have in common the opportunity for timeless influence on the kind of adult each student-athlete can become. This can occur in a variety of ways. Examples include developing and enhancing the elements of character (e.g., positivity, loyalty, and empathy); igniting the power of passion; honing various life skills (e.g., leadership, self-advocacy, drive and perseverance, time management, and effective communication); becoming goal-oriented; learning to prioritize through thoughtful decision-making; experiencing the unique emotional connectivity and bonds integral to the cohesive function of a team and learning how to embrace the individual role in a team framework; experiencing the coach as role model and mentor; performing the role of school ambassador to the world outside of campus; learning about quality standards of performance and pursuing consistency of excellence; experiencing the power and precision of sound habits; overcoming (and exploiting) mistakes, failure, and frustration; and acquiring the courage to step outside comfort zones.

While this book treats these traits and values in separate chapters, many are interrelated and feed one another. High school sports are not a static-classroom activity. They manifest through continual interactive performance in team practices and game competition. Through much of the athletic experience, the emotional, mental, and physical faculties of student-athletes are in virtually uninterrupted play and motion. Everything that occurs during the experience, whether in practice, film sessions, game competition, or other team activities, can be felt and absorbed. Every communication, whether in the form of words, nonverbal signals, or body language, reaches the team and its constituents. Evaluation and judgment of athletic performance are ongoing in tandem. There is no sneaking cell phone use or hiding or sleeping in class, other than perhaps a fleeting daydreaming or sidebar moment between teammates. The experience is all-consuming for everyone at all times and its impact pervasive and constant. It is special and distinctive.

In his recent book *Crazy-Proofing High School Sports*, John Tufte, a professor of education at the University of Mary in Bismarck, North Dakota, and former high school coach and dean of students, notes,

> The opportunities provided for student-athletes in high school sports are difficult to reproduce elsewhere. . . . Whether we in education care to embrace this reality or not, few classrooms can claim to play a significant role in improving a student's physical well-being, insisting they communicate effectively and with maturity, presenting them with opportunities to make good decisions, expecting teamwork, and helping them cope with mistakes, all within a 60-minute session.[2]

Of course, the benefits of a well-considered high school athletic program do not spring automatically or get applied with the same emphasis and effectiveness everywhere. To generate the range of available benefits, of necessity, coaches must, as teachers must in their classrooms, be skilled, run their programs conscientiously, keenly appreciate and be committed to the long-term impact of their programs on student-athletes, and implement their programs with self-awareness, humility, enthusiasm, and commitment. For their part, schools must formulate athletic programs that stand for something important to them, meaning they should be value-based.

It is true, too, that realizing the extensive benefits of a high school athletic program is not always smooth sailing. Mistakes occur. Goals and expectations require recalibration. Setbacks, reassessments, and the need for improvement are standard fare. Some lessons sink in deeper than others, and some might not manifest for a time or at all. Coaches will emphasize certain qualities and intangibles more or differently than other coaches and allocate their time differently based on their goals and priorities. Each student-athlete will have experiences that impact them in ways that sometimes differ from how their teammates experience the same circumstances. Not every athletic program is or can be the same. The challenge is what to emphasize and nurture. The process is beautifully imperfect.

Common to all, however, is a collective experience that reflects a portfolio of bountiful life lessons and intangibles that will affect them forevermore. No matter how the specifics and nuances are parsed, high school athletics present golden opportunities to help our youth both cope with a difficult, confusing, and sometimes unsettling time in their lives and fundamentally empower them to develop rich skill sets, values, and personal traits to help them navigate the many roads that await them once their educational experiences have run their course.

I hasten to note that none of what follows is intended to exalt athletics over academics. On the contrary. Academics are and should remain the embodiment of the high school experience. It is to suggest, however, that a well-developed and conscientious high school athletic program should stand shoulder-to-shoulder in the hierarchy of educational values and be a coveted component of the high school curriculum, what the National Federation of State High School Associations has called the "other half of education." Indeed, high school athletics are their *own curriculum*, with their own set of values and learning opportunities, a stand-alone syllabus that other educational activities cannot, by definition, replicate.

You might not agree with everything this book advances. You might have a different perspective here and there or prefer to emphasize or exalt other aspects of the high school sports experience. You might prefer to supplement the core tenets of this work. Some even might take the view that the smorgasbord of benefits depicted in this book is romanticized or a Pollyannaish indulgence. That is all good. The overriding goal here is to compel recognition of and inspire dialogue about how the high school experience can, in the long haul, benefit the youth we are duty-bound to serve.

It is also, I respectfully submit, no suitable answer to the admittedly difficult project I urge in this book that kids don't always listen, high school politics often impede effective coaching, or coaches have too much to do and not nearly enough time in which to do it. Each is true. But none should stand in the way of fulfilling the overall mission to teach and mentor student-athletes and get them ready for what awaits them as adults. We owe that to them. We expect much of them as athletes, and we should expect more from us. We can hardly exhort them to work hard at a sport if we don't work harder to help them become productive citizens and happy and thriving people.

This book, then, is not only a statement about the importance of high school athletics, but also a call to arms to school administrators, coaches, athletic directors, parents, and local communities to bring keener focus, greater thought, and expanded commitment to the nonsport aspects of high school athletic programs. It perhaps goes without saying that the more coaches, parents, and schools prioritize and develop the nonathletic skills, traits, and values of high school athletic programs—those that have less direct pertinence to the tally of points and goals—the richer, more meaningful, and greater the long-term impact of what student-athletes experience. As we build and implement value-based athletic programs, student-athletes will become more rounded people and be more anchored in their lives, and poised to serve our communities in a myriad of productive and positive ways.

Criticism of High School Athletics

A handful of common sense is worth a bushel of learning.

—Proverb

Looking back on my high school athletic experience, I realize that the specific games, statistics, and individual accolades did not matter for much once the time arrived to begin living a responsible and productive adult life. What mattered more than anything were how my athletic experiences in high school shaped me, how they taught me who I am, about character, and how to work effectively with others. I learned to be more responsible and accountable, how to lead when the situation called for it, and, where appropriate, how to follow and fulfill effective roles in other situations. With the benefit of hindsight, I see how the life lessons that came with competitive athletics in high school were much more than the sports themselves and prepared me to be a better person. I'm not sure I would be the same but for that athletic experience. I am immensely grateful for those opportunities and for the time and effort my coaches took to guide me and show genuine interest in my personal development.[1]

It is unremarkable to observe that high school sports have their share of challenges and low moments. Coaches sometimes lose perspective, exalting winning above all else. Parents meddle with coaches and teams, and inflict emotional harm on their children or miss opportunities to teach their children valuable lessons. Player self-interest can undermine team values and goals. Sometimes athletic programs spend too much money on certain sports

5

and overemphasize athletics, to the detriment of academics. And, on occasion, fans lose sight of their roles, cloak themselves in negativity, and even become unruly. There are other illustrations. High school sports—like most any endeavor—have their share of warts. Anyone with experience in high school sports, whether administrator, athletic director, coach, teacher, parent, player, or community member, knows this. We each have headshaking stories to share. But do these imperfections mean we should marginalize or, perish the thought, abolish high school sports? As crazy as the notion may seem, an article in a national publication suggested maybe we should.

In October 2013, the *Atlantic* published an article provocatively titled, "The Case against High School Athletics."[2] The title alone seemed a major shot across the bow, promising explosive content that would reduce the foundation of high school athletics to rubble. But as it turned out, upon examination, the disclosed content was untethered from its title. Distilled to its essence, the article was a case study of one school that had lost its way because of financial troubles and was eventually able to right itself. Beyond that, despite the far-reaching claim of its title, the piece was unworthy of consideration as serious commentary about the state of high school athletics in the United States. The following is a brief analysis.

The *Atlantic* article advanced two related arguments to bolster its "case against" high school athletics, namely, that, (1) a gross emphasis on high school sports explained why the United States lagged far behind many countries in education, and (2) high school sports were destroying academics throughout the land because student-athletes spend too much time and schools too much money on sports.

The first argument—that Americans have slipped behind educationally because we feed on a heavy diet of high school athletics—found no support in the article, as it lacked any research to support that sweeping proposition. The article was content to make that conclusory assertion, in various iterations, in the apparent hope repetition might yield credibility. The art of persuasion, however, requires more.

Furthermore, the assertion is unsupportable, as studies paint quite the different picture. For example, Rep. Mike Honda, D-California, a member of the Appropriations Subcommittee on Labor, Health and Human Services, Education, and Related Agencies, and a former teacher, school principal, and school board member, said that one of the "greatest lessons" to glean from a report of the Program for International Student Assessment is that the United States lags behind in education, not because of sports, but because of "inequity" in school resources to the detriment of "impoverished and racially isolated schools in the United States." In other words, when compared with better-performing nations, there is a conspicuous "disparity in academic performance that falls along economic and racial lines."[3]

In addition, one of the most comprehensive and most rigorous educational studies ever undertaken—the Third International Mathematics and Science Study, released by the International Association for the Evaluation of Educational Achievement—identified the following reasons for the disappointingly low international educational ranking of the United States: (1) American teachers stress "breadth rather than depth," (2) higher-performing countries have higher standards for student achievement, and (3) teachers in higher-performing countries are better prepared in pedagogical skills and spend more time working with colleagues and honing their lessons. Again, sports were not a factor.[4]

Similarly, a 2008 study by the Corporation for National and Community Service found that schools in less affluent and impoverished communities suffer educationally because of a lack of funding and other resources, and a lack of professional development. Those communities, understandably, have different and more acute priorities. Sports don't enter the equation.[5]

More fatal to the argument that high school sports have caused our educational standing to plummet internationally are the results of a study (among others) the *Atlantic* article missed, which bears specific mention because it addressed the precise theory the article advanced.

In 2013, several months *before* the publication of the *Atlantic* article, Daniel Bowen and Jay Greene, at the University of Arkansas, published the results of a study that tested "whether high schools that give greater priority to athletic success do so at the expense of academic success." In undertaking this work, Bowen and Greene had in mind the controversial work of sociologist James Coleman, whose work the *Atlantic* article mentioned. In 1961, Coleman published *The Adolescent Society*, which advanced the theory that "students involved in athletics suffered academically because of the time and energy devoted to sports."[6]

Bowen and Greene found to the contrary: "High schools that devote more energy to athletic success also tend to produce more academic success." They also found that "higher rates of athletic success and participation were associated with schools having higher overall test scores and higher educational attainment." In conclusion, they noted that their "data suggest that this claim that high school athletic success comes at the expense of academic success is mistaken" and that "it is clear that high schools that devote more energy to sports also produce higher test scores and higher graduation rates."[7]

John Tufte, in *Crazy-Proofing High School Sports*, provided anecdotal support for that empirically-based conclusion:

Leaders in education have long known that one of the best things working for academics in their schools is the presence of sports. Athletics,
through necessity alone, have served to keep students in attendance and
at least minimally proficient in the classrooms. Sports have been used as
the ultimate big brother or sister for decades, and it has often worked
marvelously.[8]

The second *Atlantic* argument—that excessive time and money devoted to
sports is sounding the death knell of high school academic programs—is
based on a single school that was the victim of *financial mismanagement*,
which purportedly caused its academic programs to regress, while its sports
programs flourished. Based on the description in the *Atlantic*, the high
school under scrutiny had lost sight of its priorities and found itself in crisis,
prompting the school to eliminate its entire athletic program. But the pre-
dicament in which that specific school found itself, of its own doing, said
nothing about the tens of thousands of high school programs that maintain
an acceptable balance between academics and athletics, and provide students
the considerable benefits of both. To be sure, the *Atlantic* article didn't say
or show anything to the contrary. Indeed, as the *Atlantic* article conceded,
once the showcased school got its academic house in order, it "brought back
a volleyball team and a cross-country team, in addition to basketball, baseball, track, and tennis."[9] Thus, the troubled school eliminated sports not as
a radical reformulation of school values or a damning of athletics, but as a
temporary solution to a problem that threatened its existence. That school-
specific experience cannot credibly be trumpeted as an indictment of high
school athletics in general.

More fundamentally, the *Atlantic* article seemed to misunderstand much
about high school athletics. It argued that high schools would be better served
if they produced one-dimensional academic student machines, whether in
math, science, English, or social studies, and that high school athletics exist
merely to "tempt kids into getting an education." Both assertions, respectfully, are off the mark.

First, high schools don't exist for students to become proficient in math
or science; their overall charter is to lay a rich groundwork so our youth can
become productive citizens. Iconic and influential writer and artist William S.
Burroughs put it succinctly: "The aim of education is the knowledge, not of
facts, but of values."[10] More recently, the National Federation of State High
School Associations (NFHS)—the existence and extensive contributions of
which the *Atlantic* article ignored—has stated,

The National Federation of State High School Associations (NFHS) and
its membership believe that interscholastic sports and fine arts activities

promote citizenship and sportsmanship. They instill a sense of pride in community, teach lifelong lessons of teamwork and self-discipline, and facilitate the physical and emotional development of our nation's youth. . . .

Activity programs provide valuable lessons for practical situations—teamwork, sportsmanship, winning and losing, and hard work. Through participation in activity programs, students learn self-discipline, build self-confidence, and develop skills to handle competitive situations. These are qualities the public expects schools to produce in students so that they become responsible adults and productive citizens. . . . Participation in high school activities is often a predictor of later success—in college, a career, and becoming a contributing member of society.[11]

Second, high school athletics promote the physical, mental, moral, social, and emotional well-being of student-athletes and specifically such lifetime values as discipline, self-advocacy, turning failure into opportunity, sportsmanship, teamwork, hard work, time management, leadership, citizenship, and character, among other skills, as discussed later in this book. And they do so, I submit, better than any math or science class ever could. Juli Doshan, an editorial assistant with NFHS, captured the point this way: "In today's high school setting, a coach is one of the most influential people in a student-athlete's life."[12] That impact tends to be timeless. People in their 60s, 70s, 80s, and even 90s still recall with remarkable indelible precision the experiences they had with their coaches. This reflects the immeasurable power of coaching and its attendant responsibility. The power coaches possess is at once scary and beautiful. Coaches who recognize and consciously exercise that power with a sharp eye toward advancing a thoughtfully conceived value-based athletic curriculum can fulfill the grander purposes of their calling as coach and mentor.

The *Atlantic* article was also silent on the extensive long-term benefits of high school athletics. The closest it came to articulating the panoply of high school athletic benefits was this: "Like any American, I can rattle off the many benefits of high school sports: 'exercise, lessons in sportsmanship and perseverance, school spirit, and just plain fun.'"[13]

For one, it is misinformed to pigeonhole high school sports as a single-dimensional, fun-generating form of physical exercise. In terms of cognition alone, high school sports are immensely challenging and require consistent use of mental faculties. Indeed, high school athletes have their own version of a textbook called the playbook, which typically includes complex material and features elements of science, art, and logic. Moreover, high school sports involve complex strategies, unique codes, distinct languages, nonverbal communication, and precise and quite nuanced applications of skill technique.

More to the immediate point, high school sports are also rich in life lessons, values, and virtues, which research repeatedly affirms. The narrow perspective of the *Atlantic* article about the benefits of high school sports turned two blind eyes to the countless studies that speak to the extensive and long-term benefits of high school athletics. There are scores of studies that establish a positive link between high school athletics and an array of educational, employment, and health outcomes, as well as overall well-being and life skills.[14]

For example, studies show that when compared with non-athletes high school athletes have higher GPAs (especially grade scores in math and science); demonstrate superior time-management and leadership skills; drop out of high school less frequently; have higher class attendance; suffer lower rates of discipline referrals and antisocial behavior; have higher self-esteem; have less emotional distress, suicidal behavior, substance abuse, and physical and sexual victimization; formulate higher attainment expectations for themselves; maintain better self-control; score higher on state assessments; graduate at higher rates; are more likely to complete a college education; participate more extensively in community activities; produce more business and government leaders; and have better physical and emotional health. Not surprisingly, the studies also establish that participation in high school athletics predicts later-life outcomes independent of other predictors, for instance, gender, race, ethnicity, and socioeconomic status, and are a school's best predictor of adult success. They demonstrate that high school athletics foster skills essential to the long-term growth and development of the mind, body, and emotional well-being of the student-athlete.[15]

As demonstrated in the pages that follow, high school athletes often have a leg up in competing for jobs. That is because the skills acquired as athletes transfer exceptionally well to the workplace. In November 2016, *Inc.* magazine published an article entitled "Five Reasons Athletes Make Superior Employees." The five reasons are as follows: (1) Athletes excel at time management; (2) they have top-flight work ethics; (3) they know how to handle adversity; (4) they are willing to learn, or in coaching parlance, they are coachable; and (5) they work well in groups.[16]

The *Atlantic* article also suggested that the United States should adopt the European model of club sports to the exclusion of high school sports. The European model features a system heavily subsidized with tax revenues, which the United States doesn't have and won't have any time soon. Those other nations provide health care and housing programs that allow their teachers to spend less time doing social work and more time on academics.[17] In *Crazy-Proofing High School Sports*, Tufte debunked the notion that we should emulate the European model:

Many ill-informed scholars in our country praise the European model, mostly for removing sports from school. . . . This is incredibly shortsighted thinking, however, for countless reasons. Simply moving sports outside of school parameters would not eliminate problems. Rather, it would make them horribly worse for the people who matter the most—the kids. . . . If high school sports in this country have taught us anything, it is that the less of an educational presence we have, the worse the experience is for everyone. Do we really want some of these "concerned" and passionate dads, with all their free time, coaching high school kids 12 months a year? Those closely associated with both education and coaching kids know better than to make the European role models for our educational and extracurricular needs. . . . The high school sports system in the United States may not be perfect, but it is the most sensible approach there is for accomplishing what wise adults know to be beneficial for young people.[18]

Furthermore, the "club" approach caters to families with disposable income and fails to account for the potent effects of poverty on academic performance, a situation worsening in the current political climate. If the author of the *Atlantic* article had her way, sports during the high school years would be for the privileged few who could afford club activities, a flaw that renders the club model regressive (wholly apart from the demonstrable inferiority of club sports to high school athletics in preparing youth for adulthood). In a rejoinder to the *Atlantic* piece, via an article entitled "High School Sports Aren't Killing Academics," Daniel Bowen and Colin Hitt referenced research based on data drawn from the National Education Longitudinal Study, noting that "reducing or eliminating these opportunities would most likely deprive disadvantaged students of the benefits from athletic participation, not least of which is the opportunity to interact with positive role models outside of regular school hours."[19] Indeed, as one coach wrote in the wake of the *Atlantic* article,

We have all heard of inner-city students whose only guidance came from a coach or a sports team. These may be at-risk kids who would have no reason to stay in school were it not for the athletic programs offered and the fact that they had to perform at minimum grade standards to participate.[20]

A former high school soccer player, now a mother of two and a swimming instructor, described that searing reality:

High school athletics changed my life. I lived in the "hood," and competing on a school team kept me out of trouble. I didn't get pregnant. I didn't get into drugs and all that crazy stuff. It kept my life together by keeping me focused on goals and making sure I did what I could to lead a good life.

What kind of job was I going to have? How was I going to feed myself? Back then, it wasn't a joke. It was life or death. Many kids in my neighborhood became gang members and got caught up in bad stuff, including drugs. But for the athletes among us, sports were our life, our ticket out of Dodge. We held on for dear life, and it kept us out of trouble. Sports in high school gave us all positive direction, discipline, and a value system, and helped build our character.

Realism also bears mention. High school sports are as popular as ever. They aren't going anywhere. The NFHS conducts an annual Athletics Participation Survey based on figures provided by its member state high school associations to demonstrate the extent to which youth participate in high school sports. As its studies consistently establish, in terms of diversity of experience alone, the selection of sports available to students is vast and increasing. The nation's high schools offer 60 different sports that are being enjoyed like never before. The NFHS recently described the pervasiveness of high school athletics today as follows:

> Led by the largest one-year increase in girls' participation in 16 years, the overall number of participants in high school sports increased for the 28th consecutive year in 2016–17. . . . Thanks to increases in all of the top 10 participatory sports, the number of girl participants reached an all-time high of 3,400,297. The increase of 75,971 from the previous year is the largest one-year jump since the 2000–01 sports participation report.[21]

There is no credible "case" to be made "against" high school athletics. Of course, a case can always be made for high schools to *improve* their athletic programs. For example, athletic programs overall can do a better job of following the lead of such impactful organizations as the Positive Coaching Alliance. Coaches can spend more time and effort on values and life lessons rather than relentlessly trying to conquer the win–loss column. Parents can do a better job of facilitating the athletic experience in positive ways rather than overprotecting and living vicariously through their children. Athletic directors can rebalance their efforts and spend more time on leadership and less time as administrative caretakers. Communities and fan bases can be more positive and supportive, and rid themselves of unacceptable behavior.

There is no credible "case" to be made "against" high school athletics.

Not to wax too philosophically, but improvement is a way of life, a continuous journey of adjustments and gives and takes that apply to most everything we do, including all aspects of educational institutions. Identifying areas of improvement in high school sports does not entail creating "cases against" our high school athletic programs. They are precisely the opposite: They are "cases *for*" athletic programs, part and parcel of the innate process of learning and change. The wonderful balance among mental, emotional, and physical well-being that high school athletics foster and the values and lifelong lessons imparted are delectable recipes for future success and contentment. We should commit to the process like never before, continuously refine the experience, and celebrate (not eviscerate) the opportunities high school athletics provide. As this book shows, the long-term benefits of high school athletics are specific, far-reaching, and enduring.

• 2 •

Self-Advocacy

Your time is limited, so don't waste it living someone else's life.

—Steve Jobs[1]

When my mobile phone rings at 10:30 p.m. in the middle of the week, I have instant dread and hope it is a misdialed number. It isn't, but it is not what I fear; it is what I totally don't expect. It is the father of a varsity player of mine, calling to let me know his daughter is in a major funk: "She's depressed, coach, and will not talk about it, and we have been unable to help her. But it plainly has to do with the team." I hadn't noticed anything unusual with her, except she had not played her best lately, which I tell him. I explain how players don't always play up to expectations, theirs and ours, but I am happy to talk to her and suggest he tell her to come see me before practice tomorrow. Then comes the rub. She doesn't know her father is calling, and if she finds out, he will have hell to pay! That comment ties my hands as far as I am concerned, but I am not willing to take him or her off the hook: "I very much appreciate your dilemma and respect your concerns. This is an important learning moment for her. You don't have to tell her you called. Yet, find a way to get her to reach out. It is important that she initiate contact with me. If she does, I will take it from there." Two days later, she approaches me at the end of practice, and we find a quiet place to talk. As it turns out, she read two recent game substitutions I made for her as punishment for less-than-stellar play and, worse, a vote of no confidence. Neither is true, and I quickly repair the misunderstanding. I assure her that my faith and confidence in her—she is our most talented player as a sophomore—remains strong and consistent. I spend most of our meeting, however, commending

15

her for taking the initiative to talk to me and exploring the importance of advocating for herself in everything she does. I urge her to reach out to me or others whenever she has concerns she believes I or they can help address.

Self-advocacy is the essence of self-determination. It fuels confidence and drive. Self-determined people are particularly adept at making decisions, setting goals, solving problems, managing their own needs, interacting with others, and performing tasks independently, a characteristic renowned psychologist Albert Bandura labeled "self-efficacy."[2] They take care of their own business. They stand for themselves.

> Self-advocacy skills are immeasurably important in the larger world student-athletes will someday explore on their own, not only in the workplace, but also in most daily events.

A common idiom applies here: A squeaky wheel gets the grease. Self-advocacy skills are immeasurably important in the larger world student-athletes will someday explore on their own, not only in the workplace, but also in most daily events. Those skills give them greater control of what happens in their lives, instill self-respect, and increase contentment through feelings of accomplishment and by being grounded. The National Federation of State High School Associations (NFHS) emphasizes the vital importance of self-advocacy, especially in the context of athletics.

Self-advocacy is heavily stressed as part of the educational experience and is reflected in many athletic department philosophies. It is an important part of a student-athlete's overall experience, according to Jeff Rudzinsky, athletic director at Marlboro High School in New Jersey. "Part of educational athletics is learning responsibility," Rudzinsky said, continuing,

> Whether it is making sure you have your uniform on game day or being able to talk to the coach about what you need to do to get on the field, a major part of that experience is learning to advocate for yourself. Coaches want student-athletes who are independent and who can think and speak for themselves.[3]

A core value for any high school athletic program to feature is self-advocacy. During a high school athletic career, occasions repeatedly arise for student-athletes to look inward (with suitable adult guidance and encouragement) and communicate their wants. The situation that most frequently implicates self-advocacy is playing time, or PT (or what I call opportunities to contribute, or OTC). Virtually every player, at one time or another, becomes unhappy about the minutes allocated to them in games. There are many other examples. Players sometimes become disenchanted with the roles coaches ask them to fill; a junior varsity player may want to know why they didn't make varsity; a senior might be curious about why they weren't selected as captain; a player might believe a coach is treating them unfairly in some specific manner; players or an entire team may raise concerns about how practice is run, propose a modification of a designed play, challenge the usefulness of a specific offensive or defensive system, or advocate for new or different equipment; or a player may want to skip practice or even a game to attend a school or family event, finish a school assignment, or study for an exam.

Coaches cannot stress enough to players and parents the importance of players taking initiative to speak up for themselves and act in their best interests. As I am fond of saying, "They can't say yes, unless you ask." Of course, they can say "no" too. The maturation process also entails knowing (and accepting) that taking initiative does not, per se, guarantee desired results. A current athletic director of a collegiate Division I program on the East Coast recalled how that reality played out when she played high school ball:

> As an athletic director, I am big on self-advocacy. It helped shape me as a young woman student-athlete in high school. I recall confronting our AD at the time about our basketball coach. I spoke up for myself in passionate terms. And while I got rebuffed, he didn't discourage me, only assured me I was mistaken in my views, which he said I would see as I got older, and I did. But the experience resonated with me for life. I felt empowered by my courage to challenge him. It is why I am who I am. I had to be a big girl and put on big girl pants, and meet with the AD. I did it, and it changed me. I am so grateful for those moments.

As a matter of team athletics, mentoring student-athletes to speak their mind and give verbal expression to what they feel, without fear of judgment or reprisal, empowers the team as well. While not every idea will survive the day and not every expressed feeling will get channeled as desired, being heard within the protective confines of a team increases individual investment in the team mission, emboldens the collective effort, and encourages further self-expression.

Sometimes student-athlete promotion is a group effort and takes the form of collaborative leadership. This happens, for example, when captains combine to help a reticent teammate take steps to express what's troubling them. Here is one such example from a former high school basketball player, now an elementary school teacher and high school and club basketball coach:

We had a new coach and a new teammate, both new to the school, and the teammate was having a rough transition. He wasn't happy with himself, his role, and how he felt the coaches were handling him. My cocaptain and I felt we needed to address the problem by bringing it to the attention of the head coach. We arranged a meeting among the four of us: coach, our teammate, and the two of us. We didn't speak for him, only tried to spearhead the conversation and present the problem for him and coach to explore. He did his own talking. As captains, we felt an obligation to provide space for our teammate to stand for himself. It was a memorable meeting, changed the course of the team dynamic the rest of the season, and affirmed the value of speaking up and taking a stand.

Sometimes a cause arises from common ground and is packaged in collective expression. Teams often gather sans coaches to discuss challenges the team is facing during their sports journey. Some coaches encourage team meetings even in the absence of major problems to ensure their teams feel invested enough in the process and encourage teammates to voice their views outside the glare of the coaching staff and exclusively among peers. Those situations tend to empower players and teams in ways otherwise unavailable.

Sometimes in the high school athletic experience, happenstance intervenes with growth opportunity. In that case, the obvious hope is that student-athletes seize the day. That is what this high school athlete did, with long-term impact:

> I recall an incident that happened in high school that changed the way I approached problem-solving. A situation developed where the team became disappointed in itself. Someone called a players-only meeting, which seemed radical. We met and hashed everything out in an open and supportive setting. The meeting built trust. But more than that it taught me the power of advocating for what I thought important. Now, if I spot an issue or identify something I'd like improved, I am inclined to seek a solution and promote a result. I find myself willing to do that more frequently, and it stems from my high school athletic experiences. I learned I didn't need the sign-off or the approval of anyone else to seek change. It is a liberating feeling.

While self-initiative can generate tangible results for student-athletes, it also cultivates the courage to seek an adult audience to hear what is on their mind. Parents play an important role here. When I was still a high school coach, my oldest son was a junior starting point guard for his high school basketball team. The team had a new coach, who was barely out of high school. He was conversant with the technical aspects of the game but too young and inexperienced to perform a mentoring role and know how best to guide his young athletes, some of whom were a mere two years younger than he. The limitations of the young coach impacted my son negatively, and as a result, the team suffered as well. Other parents, knowing I was an experienced coach, urged me a few times to intervene on my son's behalf, and as often as they did, I politely declined, telling them the situation was my son's to handle. Eventually, my son came to me in frustration seeking counsel, which I welcomed, and together we hatched a plan for him to approach the coach, him alone, which he did. The lesson was invaluable for both of us.

Even when well-intentioned, parents can be an impediment. They are known to intervene prematurely and quash the initiative of their child to take care of their own business. In 2014, NFHS published an article by Karrah Ellis entitled, "Self-Advocacy: Helping Student-Athletes Address Issues on Their Own." It spoke to this problem: "When parents intervene prematurely, this act stifles the students' ability and willingness to self-advocate," said Liza Trombley, director of English for Shrewsbury (Massachusetts) High School. "Parents are only trying to help their kids, but it is shortsighted. Forcing kids to advocate for themselves benefits them in the long run."[4]

The inclination of certain parents to step in front of their children and assume their voice is worth a pause. Those outside the emotional bubble in which parents of high school students often find themselves have the vantage point to see how parental intervention can easily jeopardize personal growth, especially the development of skills that will come in handy when their children must navigate the world outside the nest. We learn best when we are engaged in what we have to learn. Mom or dad, for instance, will not always be present or even welcome after high school when their child faces issues involving college professors, coaches, employers, romantic partners, business colleagues, commercial interactions, investors, and others. When coaches insist their players advocate for themselves, they make a significant contribution to the growth of their athletes.

The acquisition of self-advocacy skills in high school sports can find expression in the most mundane aspects of adult life. One of the powers of athletics in high school, and at other levels as well, is that its impact can be subtle. The changes the high school athletic experience can bring are not always plain. There can be a shaping of character and style beneath the surface of self-awareness that can manifest more conspicuously down the road when it is least expected, even in the simplest of situations, as this former high school soccer player shared:

> Coach never stopped preaching the importance of doing for ourselves. He never wanted our parents to "fight our battles." He insisted we speak

up for what we wanted. That did not mean we got what we wanted, as I learned, but he treated it like any other skill we practiced on the soccer pitch. That stayed with me and would come out in everyday situations. For example, it sounds almost silly, but I remember when a check I sent got lost in the mail, and I had to decide whether to wait to see if it reached its destination, taking the chance the wrong person might cash it, or process a stop payment on the check and pay a fee (which I could ill afford) and write a replacement check. I asked myself what would coach expect me to do? The answer came quickly: Go to the bank and try to persuade them not to charge me the stop payment fee, which is what I did, with success. I have learned to not always accept the cards I am dealt and seek what I feel I want or deserve.

Other times the power of self-advocacy can be uncommonly heartwarming and life-changing. Consider a dilemma facing a legally blind high school female athlete who played basketball at a high school on the East Coast about a decade ago. She literally couldn't see farther than 10 feet. This compelled her to create a new communication system so her teammates could work with her effectively and allow her to function as an effective teammate. She promoted different ways to get the job done in practice and game situations. She conscientiously set out to adjust her style of play and inspire her teammates to adjust to her, all the while serving the team mission. She knew the test she faced. She knew the challenge went beyond being a contributing team member and enjoying the experience of playing high school basketball. It was about her ability to persevere and control her destiny. By modifying her game and getting her teammates to embrace her—for example, in how she outleted a rebound and how her teammates communicated with her to accept the outlet pass—she developed a keen sense of purpose and self-advocacy, and became stronger for the experience. Now, no matter how much she is challenged in whatever she does, she knows to ask the question, "How do I get through this? I've been there before. I can do it again." High school sports empowered her to believe in herself.

Athletes entering high school often have had things done for them most of their lives. Their do-it-for-themselves skills, to the extent they exist at all, are undeveloped. High school athletics can change that in a meaningful way. High school sports programs owe student-athletes an emphasis on self-advocacy. To make full use of the opportunities to develop self-advocacy skills for student-athletes, school administrators, athletic directors, coaches, and parents must get on the same page and commit to prioritizing the importance of this vital personal skill. It is especially important for athletic directors and school administrators to support efforts of their coaching staffs to draw a line in the sand between student-athlete initiative and parental protection and coddling. Coaches deserve to have their backs protected on this vital source of learning. It is not enough, as most schools do, to have expressed policies and implementing rules that delineate protocol for communicating and advocating in a sports program. Those are essential, of course. But more than that, adults must brave the test of honoring protocols with consistent action. The growth possibilities at that age level are enormous.

• 3 •

Leveraging Mistakes and Failure

Only those who dare to fail greatly can ever achieve greatly.

—Robert F. Kennedy[1]

In consecutive tournament games, Lamont, our point guard, committed careless turnovers down the stretch that prevented us from closing out a win. In the first of the two games, he committed the same turnover in back-to-back possessions, both with less than two minutes in the game. The turnover in the second game was much the same. The two games were not his finest hours, and to say he is deflated from the experience is an understatement. He is downright dejected. Following the second game, with game three of the tournament set for the next day, we ask him to stay a few minutes after the postgame team meeting so the coaches can meet with him. Of course, we encourage him, but mostly we challenge him. We tell him he is fortunate to have arrived at a personal moment of truth, a test of how he will show up the next two tournament games. He has, we suggest, two ways to go: He can feel sorry for himself and retreat inside—as he currently is doing—or put it all behind him, rise to the occasion, become stronger for the experience, and demonstrate team leadership. The next game, he takes charge from the opening tip and leads the team to a decisive tournament win with 8 points, 6 assists, and 6 steals. The next day, during the fourth and final game of the tournament, he is even better, dominating the game with 21 points, 6 rebounds, 2 assists, and 3 steals, in another decisive win. He has proven something to himself and his teammates about the power of good mistake response.

*F*ailure is the gateway to success. When failure drops in our path, it comes with new information and opportunity. The willingness to take risk, make mistakes, and leverage missteps into advantage opens new vistas and develops courage to confront challenges of every sort. Increasingly, we as a culture are appreciating that dynamic. Still, the word *failure* bears a heavy negative connotation. Perhaps we should limit its usage or, better still, redefine its meaning, for example, failure is an initially disappointing event that holds teaching promise. Linguistics aside, as studies show, the willingness to openly examine mistakes and shortcomings with understanding and self-compassion generates personal well-being, optimism, and happiness, and reduces anxiety and depression.[2]

According to Internet entrepreneur Noah Kagan, "Roughly 86 percent of what we do fails. But eventually the 14 percent works, and that's what everyone sees."[3] The challenge is obvious: In business, as well as in sports, setbacks will occur, and sometimes when least expected. When they do, we are summoned to step back, see the larger picture, and brace for the challenge of adversity. How we persevere in the face of struggle is what earns us respect, strengthens us, makes us more resilient, and drives us to succeed at the next turn. Admitting error is not weakness; it is strength. We grow because we err. In the words of Ai Weiwei, contemporary Chinese artist, sculptor, and activist, "Maybe being powerful means being fragile."[4]

A hallmark of competitive high school athletics is the recurring opportunity to confront, manage, and leverage mistakes and failure. Competitive high school athletics place athletes consistently in situations that hold potential for adversity and disappointment. Athletes take risks every day, whether in practice or in game competition. In fact, the world of the athlete is inherently risk-taking, and athletes learn early about risk and failure in a deeply personal way. "Failure" in athletics (and elsewhere) is an opportunity to grow, refine, and enlarge existing talent and skill. Having the strength to make positive use of those situations when they arise is arguably the most powerful skill high school athletics can develop for lifetime use.

> *A* hallmark of competitive high school athletics is the recurring opportunity to confront, manage, and leverage mistakes and failure.

As found in a 2003 study by W. T. Bartko and Jacquelynne Eccles entitled "Adolescent Participation in Structured and Unstructured Activities: A Person-Oriented Analysis," published in the *Journal of Youth and Ado-*

lescence, youth who are highly involved in sport are more "psychologically resilient," that is, better able to recover from problems.[5] Take, for example, the challenge of a high school sophomore vying to become the first and only girl on a boys' varsity soccer team at a Los Angeles public school in the late 1980s, not your garden-variety high school tryout moment. The experience changed her life. Here is how she described what she faced and how she handled it:

> I can't stress enough how much value I got from soccer in high school dealing with failure and disappointment. My high school in Los Angeles didn't have a girls' soccer team. In those days, there really wasn't much interest in girls' soccer in the inner city. I could have played recreational soccer, but I wanted to play high school soccer. The level of play was light-years different. I felt it would be too convenient and easy to settle for recreational soccer. So, I went out for the boys' varsity team as the only girl trying to get a spot. To complicate matters, I was also the only non-Latino. When I arrived at tryouts, the boys kept asking me if I was "gay" or "butch." I figured that was the least of my worries and told them, straight up, "No! I just play soccer!" I made the team, but that, as it turned out, was only the beginning, as the heat got turned up. Some teammates, as well as guys on other teams, were not particularly nice. I felt like they were ridiculing me. They made inappropriate sexual comments. They hit me harder than they would anyone else, and I often felt they were trying to hurt and discourage me. Eventually, thanks in part to the coaching staff, my teammates rallied behind me and started to have my back. But it wasn't easy. Each day was a real grind. I'm not going to lie. Training with those boys kicked my ass. Some went on to play semipro and pro in Mexico and Central America. I kept going, though, and continued to extend well beyond what I thought was my comfort. But you know what? I learned you have to show up if you're going to get better. I can remember days when I thought, "I don't want to go back tomorrow. I don't feel accepted." I developed the attitude, "if you sign up, you show up." Quitting wasn't an option.

Athletes learn that failure and mistakes mostly are results of effort and are temporary, especially when used as a springboard to try something new. They learn that, throughout time, they can gain from failure as easily and often more than they can from success and that failure not only provides opportunity and informs success, it also develops humility and resilience, and sharpens focus. Moreover, they learn that final outcomes—"winning or losing"—are not the only determinates of success. They are taught the more they stumble, the more they can succeed. Athletes learn that it is easy to feel joyous and loose after a win, and that winning tests them only a little and sometimes not at all. Adversity is where character is tested and revealed. That is where the proverbial rubber meets the road.

Of course, it helps to have a coach with a well-rounded and learned perspective about what great athletes have faced and overcome. Coaches with that vantage point know what is at stake when athletes commit errors and have the chance to strengthen and redefine themselves in the process. An athletic director and coach of more than 40 years provided one such perspective, which athletes and non-athletes alike hopefully can appreciate:

> The best players I've coached made the most mistakes, and that is because they tried. They didn't care what people thought. I often use the example of professional people who have made so many mistakes. Babe Ruth held the record for the most home runs, but he also held the record for the most strikeouts. Brett Favre, now in the Pro Football Hall of Fame, threw the most touchdowns, but he also holds the record for most interceptions. The greatest play in San Francisco football history is "The Catch," but people forget Joe Montana threw three interceptions that game. Yogi Berra, when he struck out, would say, "There must be something wrong with the bat." The great ones get right back up, and that is what makes each of us a champion, in any context, when we get back up. How bad do you want it? Do you want to get up? Do you want to stay down? How important is it?

Coaches can lead the way on how to use failure and error as opportunity. They can be quick to admit mistakes of their own—we sure make enough of them—and apologize where appropriate. They can, in a word, model the behavior they want their athletes to emulate. In *Crazy-Proofing High School Sports*, John Tufte talked about the nature of the role schools play in helping youth handle disappointment in high school sports:

> The new job of educators . . . is to help our community members understand that high school sports [are] still one of the best providers of life lessons available in this country. Love, furthermore, is necessary, but not how many of us perceive it. We are not helping our adolescents if our love is an attempt to shield them from athletic disappointments. . . . High school sports are exactly where young people should be failing. This is the greatest preparation for real life that many of our kids will ever face. Failure and disappointment? It is inevitable in sports and life. Teaching perspective, moreover, is about helping our young people handle these difficult realities.[6]

In that passage, Tufte made an excellent point about the safety net of the high school sports environment. The education institutional structure protects student-athletes from the kind of severe consequences that attend real-life missteps. The high school sports venue represents an open invitation to push hard and make mistakes—without worry about anything major befalling the athlete, save a bruised ego or blemished pride. It is an environment ideally suited for making mistakes and learning from them without much risk and, in the process, getting prepared for the adult world.

James Thompson, founder of the Positive Coaching Alliance, described it this way in *Developing Better Athletes, Better People*: "Many people think struggle is a bad thing. Struggle is a *good* thing, and there is no better place for kids to learn to struggle, adapt, and overcome when things don't go well than high school and youth sports" (emphasis in original).[7]

A former high school cross-country and basketball player learned from his scholastic days to put setback in proper life perspective:

> The idea of winning and losing is a really important concept not only for kids to understand, but for adults as well. We forget there's only one team at the end of the season that will enjoy the ultimate happiness: the team that wins it all. Every other team ends their season with a loss. But how those hundreds of teams experience their season-ending loss is an important lesson. We're not all going to get the job we want. We're not all going to get the house we want. I didn't get into all the graduate schools to which I applied. The list goes on. Sports prepare you for those setbacks. All teams lose games and some more than others obviously. Learning to deal with disappointment is central to the high school athletic experience. You learn you can fail and come out on the other side okay, or even better. That was an important lesson for me.

Parents play a pivotal role in helping their kids embrace trial and error as opportunities. Unfortunately, they can look to blame others, especially coaches, for shortcomings. It is incumbent on us to reverse the direction of that tendency. One parent who raised four athletes and has an athletic background herself spoke succinctly to the long-term value of failure as a learning source, saying, "I cannot overstate how much team sports helped my kids grow up by learning to deal positively with both success and failure." Coaches also have endless opportunities to help athletes define success in nontraditional ways, one of which is the bounce-back situation. Another related pithy comment, this time on the influence of her coach, came from a former soccer player: "The philosophy of my high school coach was if you screwed something up, keep going."

Consider this e-mail I sent to one of my teams after an impressive game performance on the heels of a tough (and deflating) late-season loss:

> Gentlemen, it is easy to walk with a proverbial bounce in your step when things are going well and according to design. But the real test of maturity, the most revealing way to know whether you are ready for the next challenge,

is seeing what happens when things take a disappointing turn. "Easy" is superficial fun, for, in truth, it does little in the long-term for us and certainly does not help us become who we can be. The true test occurs when you must find a way to get off the ground after a stumble and say, "I am primed more than ever to go again."

One former athlete, now a high school coach and schoolteacher, described the process of teasing success out of failure during his high school sports experience as finding "value in small victories":

We didn't win any championships. We weren't a particularly memorable team. We don't have any banners in the gym. But we did have small victories. When I look back, I think of those moments, not game results, but the ability to compete and find silver linings in what others may decry as defeat. It came down to perspective about what you're doing. It became about taking pieces from each game and each practice, and putting it together, whether distilling to a successful move in a game or being able to run a play as a team effectively. Those were small victories. As an adult, coaching or teaching in the classroom, I try to harness those moments to teach perspective from the vantage point that things aren't always going to go well in life. I now think back to my high school team as successful because we were able to achieve an assortment of many of those less-than-grand things.

Here is how a former football player, now an investment portfolio manager, learned to put "losing" in perspective after his storied football program, which had won more than 40 consecutive games, abruptly hit the skids with a 0–11 season:

We had all these rituals in the community surrounding each football game. Each game, we visited the gravesite of the legendary coach who led the program for decades and had recently died, after which we had dinner at the current coach's house. We participated in a ritual on the five-yard line of the football field, and [in] games, where if you were starting in varsity, you wore a red shirt. In addition, the cheerleaders decorated cars, and we'd wear our jerseys to school. The school decorated the lockers and made baked goods. After games, families hosted gatherings for parents and players. It was like the entire town was involved in the process. The energy of the program and the spirit in the community were extraordinary and carried us through the doldrums of losing every week. When you have a culture with built-in values, with everyone in the town pulling in the same direction, you realize there are more important things than winning a football game.

Coaches often give their athletes specific tools to use when beset by failure or error. Each coach has their peculiar style, including code words, for handling mistake and frustration. One former high school basketball player shared how her coach got the team to use a few choice words to manage the process of moving past error, a method initially received as odd but that has stayed with her as an adult, often the way with high school athletics:

> At first, most of us thought coach's constant refrain to "flush it" weird, but over time we understood what she meant and why she harped on it so much. She was big on moving on to the next moment quickly when things didn't go well and using the mistake or frustration to create something better in the moments to come. She insisted that mistakes often were good things and that the test of a true competitor was the ability to use errors to improve and become a better teammate. I will never forget the game where I made some bad mental blunders in the first half of a game that unnerved me. Coach didn't pull punches and told me at halftime that nobody but me was obsessing or even thinking about my mistakes, and that the team needed me to "flush it" and get my head back on my shoulders. She was a little harsh, and my immediate reaction was to brood. But I eventually got it, and the lesson has stayed with me ever since. I use the "flush it" mantra whenever I get frustrated or stumble and then try to take advantage of the opportunity or at least move on with no fuss.

A high school lacrosse goalie, now a budding entrepreneur, described his equivalent of the "flush it" technique for dealing with game setbacks, which was a routine he developed for dealing with rising frustration whenever the other team slipped a shot by him for a goal:

> I would step out of my place, rip a little piece of grass out of the ground, and kind of use that to represent tossing away that last goal. So, five seconds after that goal, I was done with it. I'd scream, I'd tear a little piece of grass, and I was done with it. That same mindfulness applies to business. There are so many disasters and hiccups in starting a new business. It's like a race car driver—if I focus on the wall, I'm going to drive into it. Your car goes where your mind goes. So, basically, if I'm focusing on these disasters or setbacks, I'm going to have a lot of disasters. But focusing on the next shot as opposed to the one that just got in is the way to get to the finish line.

High school athletes, like each of us, will have their share of opportunities after formal education to confront failure and disappointment. Each time they do they will be tested. Because of their high school athletic experience, they will have the advantage to employ skills they acquired from the constant scaling of steep mountains as competitive athletes. They will be able to call on the same courage and resilience that pulled them through when competing in sports. A former high school rower and wrestler echoed this nicely:

> I think one of the biggest assets I gained from high school was not to be intimidated by problems, but be inspired by them and treat them as opportunities. I used to fear failure and now don't. You kind of seek it, because if you reach failure, you pushed a limit. Whether it's a mental barrier or a physical barrier, the only way to reach past your barriers is to try to push past them. In high school, seeking that failure was something that I learned was okay. Failing was part of the process. And then you get better and better, so that's the connection there. In every situation I've been in almost, something has gone wrong, right? What are our options based on the best information I have? And how do I solve this problem? Athletics prepare you for those moments. They teach very valuable lessons because something is going to go wrong. It's inevitable. Something is going to happen at some point in time, and we have to confront mistakes and failure.

The obstacles to success kids face in high school sports can get personal. Athletes are expected to perform in accordance with expectations and rules, and when they don't ring the bell, coaches, parents, and teammates are not shy about letting them know. This can be delicate and places a premium on communication skills—as explored in a later chapter—but being on the receiving end of feedback about performance is a separate learning moment that recurs in the often emotionally charged athletic experience. Student-athletes are challenged to receive this species of commentary in ways that help them grow. Feedback sometimes seems nonstop. Coaches are wired to succeed, and teaching moments flow like white rapids with no end. Indeed, one of the many coaching challenges is to know how to allocate time for teaching moments. Coaches must learn to prioritize, and no matter how they do it, they must understand that each teaching moment, whether team, small group, or individual, is precious for the impact potential it holds.

One characteristic of the competitive environment in high school is that, by and large, self-pity is not tolerated when mistakes are made. The athletic experience can be vigorous, with fast-moving parts. Athletes are often challenged to have thicker skin than what they sported entering high school. The following came from a former soccer player on whom that lesson was not lost:

> High school sports teach that sometimes things won't go your way and how to handle criticism when they don't. I see all the time in the business world how people take feedback personally. I understand that feeling at a base level, but as a high school athlete, I didn't feel I had that luxury. We

were expected to learn from mistakes and got the message quickly that no benefit comes from sulking. If I messed up, I was expected to double down and keep on trucking. I didn't always relish the pressure—I was a teenager after all—but I now appreciate how much it strengthened me to overcome setbacks. High school sports taught me not to take things personally. The team had a mission, and everyone tried to be honest about your flaws to achieve team goals.

To round out this discussion, consider this compelling and inspirational story of failure from a high school swimmer who dreamt of competing in the Olympics:

I think failure in sports is independently important. It's a constant, and you must figure out what it means and grow from it. My biggest high school goal was to make the Olympic Trials. I participated in various meets to get there. I kept failing. The repeated setbacks were difficult to swallow because I felt like I was doing everything I was supposed to do. I was training and executing the right way, and working as hard as I could. I was being tested big time. Each failed swim meet I had to dig deeper for strength and belief. I couldn't afford to feel sorry for myself. I had to feed off the fire of my competitive self and find the motivation to keep climbing. I redoubled my efforts at practice, drank more water to be sufficiently hydrated, and ate better. I made sure I got enough sleep. After 11 consecutive failed meets, I felt done. I had given it my best shot. Then, my coach found a 12th meet in Manhattan on the next to the last day to register. I agreed to give it a go. There were two swims that day. I didn't have to compete against anyone but myself. I had to record a great time, a personal best to qualify for the Olympic Trials. The first swim went well. I made my best time. But it wasn't good enough. I was upset. I talked to my coach, and he asked if I wanted to try again, and I said, "I don't think so. I'm going to be more tired. That was the best I can do." He said, "Why don't you cool your body down"—to get rid of the lactate—and "let's talk again in 20 minutes." After 20 minutes, I recaptured my resolve and decided to give it one final shot. I had an hour-and-a-half break, and I had a timed trial set up, me in the lane, nobody else. The entire spectator stands, filled to the top, would be watching me swim by myself in the race of my life. It was me against time. I remember midway through the swim thinking this is the most painful thing I'd ever done and I was going to remember it for the rest of my life. Further along, the pain increased, but I couldn't entertain doubt or self-pity; I forged forward. That swim was a culmination of the prior 11 meets. I finally touched the wall and recorded a new personal best and qualified for the Olympic Trials. Now I think, if I can do that, in the real world what can't I do?

James Joyce is credited with saying, "Mistakes are the portals of discovery," an adaption from his seminal work *Ulysses*. We can debate the breadth of its meaning in its literary context, but I imagine Joyce meant at base that errors are full of chances to learn. That much seems incontrovertible. But mistakes during a high school athletic career—and every athlete experiences a bevy of them—go much deeper and delicately into the learning portal. The intensity of the athletic experience, with months and months of daily hard work and continuous emotional tension, means that when mistakes are made, when failure drops on the path, it is occasion for self-introspection, a gateway to knowing more about the person, in addition to the athlete. High school sports stand alone in the high school curriculum in providing a plethora of these penetrating moments. It is one of the richest parts of the high school athletic tapestry.

· 4 ·

Goal-Setting

The greater danger for most of us isn't that our aim is too high and we miss it, but that it is too low and we reach it.

—Michelangelo[1]

Both my sons played high school varsity basketball, using personal goals each year to motivate and hold themselves accountable. One, a point guard, was keenly focused on his assist-to-turnover ratio, the only statistic he cared to have tracked for him every game. While he was touted for his defensive leadership, he felt his contributions were greater whenever he created opportunities for teammates to improve and succeed. As a senior, he averaged more than 11 assists a game, as good as most anywhere, and recorded an impressive assist-to-turnover ratio of almost 4 to 1. My other son, a shooting guard, wanted to excel at the foul line and, toward that end, developed an extracurricular program of shooting two sets of 50 foul shots a few days every week outside of practice. He regularly charted misses and makes, and increased the frequency of the routine whenever he did not achieve interim goals. In his three varsity basketball seasons, he shot 87 percent, 89 percent, and 92 percent, respectively, from the foul line.

Goals are vehicles that propel us forward. They provide sustained focus and motivation; help distinguish between strengths and weaknesses; and thus enhance self-awareness, render challenges manageable, prioritize what is important, inspire belief in self and build confidence through achievable goals, develop organizational and time management skills, and, importantly, hold us accountable. Goals are our personal life compasses.

Research shows that people who set goals succeed more than those who don't. In most any organization, goals measure success, inspire leadership and team cohesion, and empower management and employees. In education, student goals improve academic performance, instill pride, improve self-confidence, facilitate college choices, and help prepare for future challenges.[2]

> *G*oals are our personal life compasses.

Setting goals is integral to high school athletics and a skill student-athletes can easily develop. Athletic goals fuel short-term motivation and help formulate long-term vision. The goals of student-athletes need not be grandiose. They can be and often are articulated in small, incremental steps, a format that provides greater opportunity for success and reward.

Fundamentally, there are specific types of goals that a high school student-athlete can consider: (1) process, (2) forward-looking, (3) performance, and (4) outcome.

Process goals focus on small tasks within the control of the athlete and plunge the athlete into the present moment. Examples include hitting the weight room twice a week, watching game film two hours a week, or taking 90 minutes of extra batting practice at a public batting cage on weekends. These types of goals create proficiency routines and constitute a means to support and attain skill development whether short-term, intermediate, or long-term.

Forward-moving goals encase aspirations. They are, by definition, far-reaching. An extreme example is a high school athlete who wants to play professionally. While that goal may be reasonably within the reach for an exceedingly narrow group, for the overwhelming majority, it is not. Encouraging forward-looking goals at the high school level can be a touchy undertaking, as they can have a high incidence of nonachievement. While coaches don't want to discourage dreams that have some prospect of being realized, when the goal has a pronounced lack of realism, it should undergo candid vetting before an athlete embarks on an ambitious program of that nature. That way, at least, the athlete has a keen understanding of the risk–reward and enjoys frank input from knowledgeable people.

Outcome goals are typically long-range finales, a prize or a big picture item, as it were. Athletes typically have limited control of outcome goals. They can run the gamut from getting selected captain, making the varsity team as a sophomore, or getting voted athlete of the year or league MVP, among others.

For that reason, outcome goals provide an extra infusion of motivation, as the athlete must overcome various obstacles in pursuit of the end game. Take, for example, this challenge for a teenager with great ambition:

> I decided that I would like to make the Olympics in 2012, and in high school I took six months off to figure out my life and what I was going to do. The experience made me a well-rounded person. Once I returned to the pool in earnest, I trained twice a day, sometimes as many as five hours a day. Having school to preoccupy me, not just sitting around waiting for the next practice to start, was helpful to my development not just as an athlete, but also as a person. In swimming, it's, "I go this time. You go that time." You can measure performance easily, and I really like that because I felt that all the work I put in translated to my time. I gave 100 percent all the time, which I knew would translate into results at the end of the season. The work translated into something to be proud of, or if not proud of, something to reflect on why you didn't achieve your goal. I felt our coaches were good at explaining and setting benchmarks. Everything we did got measured. Now, that continues to be my motivation in all that I do. I'm motivated to get the best staff and make sure they're motivated, and I use a similar benchmark system I used as an athlete. I have directly transferred the athletic goal model to my job.

Performance goals encompass specific measurable results. Examples include setting a school record in the high jump, leading the league in kills in volleyball, or increasing a NTRP rating by .5 during the current season in tennis. Process and performance goals are often linked tightly to one another because they are easily measured. Performance goals are usually more effective than outcome goals because athletes have greater control over them. The main challenge here is identifying realistic and achievable goals, whether technical, tactical, mental, or physiological.

For their part, coaches work with athletes to ensure goals are described with specificity, an important and sometimes subtle part of the process. Otherwise, the kind of dialed-in focus so crucial to optimal performance can be diffused. For example, rather than articulating a goal of improving shooting mechanics, a basketball player might specify working to perfect the head pause before the shot, adjusting the position of the elbow in the shooting arm, or improving the resilience of the wrist snap in the shot release. Or, rather than the goal of taking a few seconds off a swim time, a swimmer might craft the specific goal of improving a flip turn or changing the up-and-down motion for the sprint flutter kick (which, in turn, might shave seconds off race time). The greater the specificity, the more precise the focus and the greater the chances the athlete will realize positive change.

How student-athletes select their goals is an important part of the goal-setting process. Self-motivated goals give the athlete ownership and a deeply personal stake in the outcome. Top-down adult influence or control can compromise or undermine the process. Incompatibility between parent and student-athlete when it comes to delineating athletic goals can be a recipe for disaster, or at least cause major frustration and emotional damage. Furthermore, while not necessary, writing down goals—in positive language—and creating benchmarks for success are good checks on goal attainability and fuel the commitment to achieve them. The process of memorializing goals is also an effective way to identify what is important to the athlete and outline what is within their control, a separate value discussed in a later chapter. It also might make sense for athletes to share goals with others to assure accountability and increase motivation.

Goal-setting in athletics is different than in the classroom, which tends to be measured in linear terms. The process of setting and seeking to accomplish goals in sports at the high school level requires a constant review along a continuum and a fair amount of give and take. It is an evolving process. As one high school coach pointed out,

> Goal-setting is a progressive thing. But it must be realistic and include self-appraisal. With grade inflation, which goes on in the classroom, it's difficult. In athletics, you must know who you are. You've got to know your level and how you match up. If you're unrealistic about it, you will have major difficulty developing, which might lead to negativity. Kids sometimes think they're better than they are, and, sometimes, they don't think they're as good as they are. If they're unrealistic, they play badly, get grumpy, don't know where they fit in, and don't know how they can be useful as a team member. In short, they will feel they have failed.

Realistic and vigilant goal-setting in high school sports can pay long-term dividends, as it did for this two-sport high school athlete:

> My participation in high school sports really helped me learn how to be competitive, set goals, and work hard to achieve them. The biggest thing I gained was focusing on setting realistic goals. Every high school kid comes in dreaming of playing in the NBA, going to the Olympics, or playing in the NFL, whatever it is. But you come to realize, maybe that's not the most realistic goal and you should focus instead on the specific steps to achieve realistic goals. It forced me to be smart about my future direction. Now if I have something I want to achieve, I think carefully about my options, assess them realistically, and identify a path to success.

Especially important in achieving goals in an athletic program are time management skills, which coaches are keen to underscore throughout the season. Time management requires balance and the ability to handle various and sometimes competing demands so the student-athlete is not overwhelmed and stressed. As student-athletes learn to manage their time efficiently, they develop good habits, with lifetime potential. Not surprisingly, three separate studies have shown that adolescents who participate in sports demonstrate improved skills in goal-setting and time management, and that these skills transfer from sports to academics, family life, and the work environment.[3]

The habit-forming component of goal-setting implicates discipline, which is integral to long-term goal achievement and, if a student-athlete is conscious enough, a sense of urgency. The following is how a former high school basketball player described it: "My high school basketball experience introduced me to discipline in goal-setting. It was a discipline that said, 'Hey, if you really appreciate this, and you recognize that it won't be here forever, be disciplined about it. Do it the right way. Set specific goals and go after them.'"

Of course, not every athlete at the high school level is a self-starter who walks into the gym, strolls onto the field, or jumps into the pool with a comprehensive mindset of goals to mark their athlete career. That is where the coach enters. Still, a coach might not get everyone to embrace the process of setting goals each year. But most athletes will and thus find themselves intricately involved in the developmental process of goal-setting. To maximize success, coaches and parents can be instrumental in getting student-athletes to focus on setting goals. Like they have with most everything else during the teenage period of life, adults with direct access to student-athletes hold a special charter to facilitate the athletic experience in a way that maximizes the learning, and goal-setting is no exception.

The key is implementing a routine consistent with how student-athletes are expected to perform and function. It is, in the end, as discussed in chapter 19, all about culture and the habits that express the values of a program. If schools want enduring impact, whatever they introduce can't be casual or irregular. The methods and standards have to be ingrained in the program. This former high school basketball player had the good fortune of participating in such a culture, which gave him the impetus to apply what he learned as an adult:

> How can I forget? Every year, coach made us sit down and make a list of goals, both short-term and long-term, individual and team. He also insisted we post the lists somewhere, like in our locker at school or at home, as a constant reminder. I'm not sure everyone posted the lists, but we were each held accountable for tracking progress. I have been much more goal-oriented ever since. I don't always make lists of goals, but I set them all the time. For example, in entering college, I was thinking about getting into government and figured law school would be a good path, after which I could hopefully find some entry position in local government for starters.

I even called coach to discuss the situation. We explored options and the challenges for each. As a short-term goal, he suggested I identify some government or law courses in college to test my appetite and, if the classes felt right, apply to law school and see what it brought. I took the college classes, went to law school, got my JD degree, and dabbled in government positions for a while. I wound up in private practice, where I am happy.

Sometimes setting the bar high can be a life-changer. It doesn't always happen on such a grand scale, of course, but when it does, the results can be far-reaching. Here is a situation where a high school soccer player used her athletic experience to chart future decision-making and goal-setting in a significant way:

I set my eye on making that boys' varsity team, a radical notion for a girl back then, and I did it. I wasn't going to settle for second best. I set my goal on what I wanted and did it. I then applied that attitude to college. I wanted to go to NYU. It was the number one school in the country for clinical social work. And I needed a scholarship. I wasn't settling, crazy as it now seems. I applied only to NYU. I wanted to be there. That was my goal. Just like making the soccer team. I got the scholarship. I live my life that way all the time. What is the goal, and how do I get there?

Top-down leadership in a high school sports program—beginning with the athletic director and the coaching staffs—is situated to develop a goal-oriented culture that offers a wide range of ways to measure growth and success, both team and individual, and monitor progress and interact effectively to make appropriate adjustments. Of all the benefits high school athletics produce, goal-setting skills are the easiest to facilitate and develop. It is a matter of commitment, organization, and diligence. The opportunities for student-athletes to become effective goal-setters for the future are manifest at this level—and achievable.

Conquering the Comfort Zone

Comfort is the enemy of achievement.

—Farrah Gray, author, columnist, and motivational speaker[1]

As a middle school coach, a mantra of mine—in honesty, a nag—is using the "weak" hand. One player resists regularly, preferring the comfy confines of old (and limiting) habits. I do not relent and begin to halt practices to make the point. Eventually, she steps outside her comfort zone and begins to attempt finishes at the basket on the left side of the floor with her left hand, despite an initial period of conspicuous awkwardness. A few years later, when she is in high school and I am coaching at a league-opponent high school, I scout her team in a preseason game. The game is close the entire way and comes down to the final possessions. With the score tied with less than 30 seconds to go, her team is defending and thus needs a defensive stop and a score to prevail. They cause a turnover and move quickly down the floor. She receives an outlet pass near mid-court and storms to the basket, angling to the right (her strong side). A defender, however, is in hot pursuit on her right, which forces her to protect the ball by switching dribbling hands, and as she does, she moves to the left side of the floor to create an advantageous angle to attack the basket. As the defender closes in, she seals the defender with her body and deftly finishes with the left hand with mere seconds left, notching a thrilling victory. After the game, we share a light moment, as I chide her about comfort zone coaching lessons gone by.

The comfort zone is a security blanket that keeps us warm and safe. It is, however, also a place bounded by mental barriers to initiative. Someone once said, "Life begins at the end of our comfort zones." That may be hyperbolic, but the point is well taken: Playing it safe generates little reward and impedes growth. Success often commands an ability to find comfort in being uncomfortable.

Ran Zilca, in *Psychology Today*, said this about comfort zones:

> We live in a society where comfort has become a value and a life goal. But comfort reduces our motivation for introducing important transformations in our lives. Sadly, being comfortable often prohibits us from chasing our dreams. Many of us are like lions in the zoo: well-fed but sit around passively stuck in a reactive rut. Comfort equals boring shortsightedness and a belief that things cannot change. Your comfort zone is your home base, a safe place not to stay in, but to return to, after each exhausting and exhilarating expedition through the wilderness of life. Take a look at your life today; if you are enjoying a shelter of comfort, break through it and go outside, where life awaits.[2]

Taking leave of personal comfort zones is a worthy end in and of itself. The benefits of stepping outside the stubborn edges of comfort are many: (1) challenging ourselves to perform at peak; (2) becoming comfortable with risks that help us grow and, equally so, being willing to fail; (3) inspiring us to be more creative; (4) aging better and staying sharp; (5) facing and overcoming fear, especially of the unknown; and (6) giving us more life choices and identifying paths that allow us to evolve continuously.

*S*uccess often commands an ability to find comfort in being uncomfortable.

Challenges to move beyond the inhibiting parameters of our comfort zones crop up in many real-life situations and many forms, for example, having difficult conversations with people we care about, changing a workout routine, changing any entrenched daily routine, starting a business, taking lessons to develop a new skill (like playing an instrument or learning a foreign language), admitting fault, revisiting long-standing points of view, doing unfamiliar or uncomfortable volunteer work, going on an adventurous trip (e.g., kayaking in rapids), and so on.

In addition, career reinvention is no longer an anomaly. It is commonplace and increasingly essential to continue having enjoyable, productive, and satisfying lives. Reinvention requires a willingness to take risk and venture into the unknown, and is insurance against stagnation. Furthermore, job security is more fleeting than ever. Individual utility in almost any career path can have a shelf life. That is not to say people can't succeed with a prolonged career, only that the comfort zone is increasingly giving way to the need to explore what else can be.

Comfort zone challenges are front and center in high school athletic programs. Conscientious athletic programs attack comfort zones with a vengeance, as coaches tend to be tireless in trying to get athletes to venture beyond their comfy habits and learn to tolerate, if not enjoy, discomfort, both mental and physical. At Point Guard College (PGC), a preeminent basketball leadership program in the United States, PGC head Dena Evans is fond of saying, "Temporary inconvenience, permanent improvement." Instinctively, especially if lacking in adventure, high school athletes often prefer the environment they know and what they are used to doing. Old habits die hard. Accepting the challenge to break down the barriers of easy street is no mean feat for any young athlete. Coaches are well-served to remind players they essentially have two paths to follow when it comes to improvement: suffer the sting of discipline or the sting of performance regret.

The threshold awareness for high school athletes is that high school sports culture differs from middle school in various ways, not the least of which is student-athletes are expected to earn opportunity. The egalitarian model of past youthful days is over. In high school, student-athletes are expected to dig deeper and work harder for what they want, unlike what was expected of them before. In high school, the word *earn* becomes a coaching standby players probably tire of hearing, but it is one of the best things any adult can say to them at that time of their lives. Entitlement has no place in a progressive high school athletic program.

Getting that message across is one of the first compelling items most coaches place on their agenda for incoming athletes, a wake-up call that bears repeating throughout the athletic campaign. The enlightenment that it is time to earn what is available doesn't always go down easily—hard work calculated to succeed is a learned habit—but it is an important growth moment for athletes, cognitively and emotionally, and essential to the maturation process. The world is more competitive than ever. Success in the postschooling environment requires getting after it, as they say, and the sooner student-athletes embrace that stark reality, the sooner they will ground themselves emotionally and be prepared for arduous challenges ahead. A longtime tennis and basketball coach offered the following insightful words on the subject:

> As a coach, one of first things I try to get kids to understand is that in high school athletics, there is no coddling and no resting on laurels. Athletes are

expected to challenge themselves, and probably in ways that are foreign to them. Individually, it is about steady development, which means fostering good habits, getting rid of bad ones, and trying new and, yes, more difficult ways to become a better athlete. We encourage the athletes to take themselves seriously, and that means, among other things, that entitlement starts to end. We try to get them to see that at some point in their lives, they can't escape competing for whatever their goals are and that opportunity will not be handed to them. Guaranteeing things like playing time is nice, because everyone gets a chance, and it breaks through the favoritism, which is common at the lower levels. But that is not what high school is or should be about. They need to know how results happen. They happen only by enduring the pain of change and getting outside comfort zones. Of course, the dynamics vary. Different kids need a different amount of work to get to the same level. Differences begin to emerge, and as they do, challenges do as well. Competition takes on a different feel and taste. And the better an athlete gets, the more they see there is to learn. And that is the second breakthrough; when people get bitten by the bug, they discover that it's infinite—there's no place to stop. And the minute you stop, you regress.

In sports, leaving the comfort zone can take many forms. This can mean spending more time practicing less-developed skills no matter how uncomfortable, as in the opening scenario to the chapter; pushing through the "burn" in a tough workout; playing a new position or role for a team; being willing to endure greater contact in competitive play; practicing with more intensity and focus; changing bad eating habits; and communicating differently and better. It is essential to growth that high school athletes discard inhibiting old habits, which is why coaches do whatever they reasonably can to inspire, nudge, and push athletes to enter the once-forbidden zones of the unfamiliar so they may progress.

Sometimes, the sharp parameters of a comfort zone can be destructive, and finding ways to overcome them can be essential to securing major life change. Consider the comments of a high school coach, whose program is known for developing the entire athlete, regarding the importance of attacking the comfort zone when character is on the line:

> Here is a more extreme example of compelling a player to find a place outside his comfort zone. The athlete in question was a prima donna and would often drag his ass in practice with a chip on his shoulder. It was a comfortable place for him. He apparently felt entitled to presume a major role on the team. He was talented, no question, and for that reason had been used to getting what he wanted in middle school and club ball. The head coach had him sit on a chair for a week watching the team practice. Coach wanted him to see what hard work looked like. He wanted him to get a close look at players working to earn opportunity. After a week, coach allowed him back,

and he came out like a raging bull. He practiced and played exceptionally hard. He held his tongue and committed to the process. He acted as if he had something to lose and much to gain. The lesson was that sometimes we need to change the script. The player later recounted that the experience, harsh as it was, was an important turning point in his life. He didn't like it at the time; in fact, it angered him. But he came to appreciate the fact that we, as a coaching staff, made an early and firm statement to him about our expectations and what he needed to do to grow.

Comfort zones are not inert configurations; they are moving targets. As athletes improve, the boundaries of their potential shift, and as they do, so do expectations. Complacency in any athletic program is a breeding ground for mediocrity. A player of mine, in a speech he gave at a school assembly that honored graduating seniors, thanked me for "never being satisfied," which he said freed him to pursue new heights despite the angst he suffered in the process of changing habits. He learned to set the bar high and never undersell his potential. Another player of mine echoed a similar sentiment, applying his risk-taking in high school sports to his responsibilities as a businessperson:

> High school sports filled me with a sense of courage. They made me more comfortable trying new things and taking risks. I now appreciate the risk–reward dynamic. It was constantly in play in high school. Our coaches challenged us to step outside the box to discard old habits in favor of new ones, knowing that pain and frustration would be the price we had to pay for what we were earning down the line. Now, whenever I enter a new or different situation in life or if I must give a presentation and get nervous, where there's a lot of pressure, I think about how I conquered challenges playing ball.

It is, of course, never easy to measure the direct relation between risk-taking in high school and bold initiative in adulthood. Sometimes it is a feeling of courage absorbed during those youthful days that never leaves. Sometimes, there is a continuum of learning with new experiences that build on foundations laid during early lessons. Sometimes the impact is direct and indelible, as shown by the following comments of a high school football player who went on to become a successful investment portfolio manager:

> High school football introduced me to how to deal with the fear of the unknown. Relatively early in life, we each get responsibilities at school and around the house, but they all feel a little bit more negotiable, or at least they did to me. But the responsibilities I had to my teammates were an entirely different matter. They were nonnegotiable. We were expected to move beyond where we felt comfortable to serve the team mission and better ourselves. It was a firm, inherent, and unmovable expectation. Before high school, playing football had been relatively easy. It was fun. And then

the stakes got raised. I had to adjust. I had to conquer the fear of pain and not meeting expectations. There is nothing more miserable than 110 degrees and 100 percent humidity, and having to run wind sprints until you can't see straight. I dreaded it until I was able to figure out how important it was to the overall goals, how essential it was as part of the process. It took me time. Life is full of challenges, and being able to draw on the experiences of having done that in the past since a relatively young age in a structured environment where you have teammates and coaches you trust is powerful. That adrenaline can-do and must-do rush never goes away. I work hard in the finance industry, but the long, sleep-deprived hours and stress are tame compared to what I suffered through and eventually mastered in high school.

Kathy Caprino, who covers career and personal growth, leadership, and women's issues, recently contributed an article on comfort zones to *Forbes* magazine entitled "Six Ways Pushing Past Your Comfort Zone Is Critical to Success." Her opening salvo captures the long-term value that high school athletes have to gain when they conquer their comfort zones:

> I've seen that one of the most damaging things you can do in your career is to stay for years where you're comfortable. I've done it, and what often ensues is that you begin to doubt your value in the marketplace and wonder if you really have the chops to succeed and thrive outside your current job. I've learned too (the hard way) that no job is secure. The only thing that is secure in life is you—your spirit, your heart, your talents and gifts, and your ability to contribute at a high level to something that matters to you in life. When you live from that knowledge and experience, you'll find (and create) gainful, rewarding work no matter where you go, despite the turbulence around you. And to do that, you need to continually push yourself out of your comfort zone.[3]

Relegating comfort zones to starting points requires constant looks inward to test readiness for scaling barriers to the other sides of talent and abilities. Four years of high school athletic competition, sometimes in multiple sports and most times for long stretches of the calendar year, bear a richness of growth opportunity not available anywhere else in the high school experience. High school sports challenge student-athletes to be bolder, more risk-adverse, and grow emotionally to fill potential. The process is (and should be) fun, but it is one of the most difficult things a student-athlete will do in high school. The responsibility for navigating the arduous road that spawns such growth is not only on the athlete. Coaches, team leaders, and parents bear some responsibility to encourage, challenge, and exhort the student-athlete to avoid the easy and embrace the hard so they can make a spirited run toward ever-changing personal heights.

· 6 ·

The Power of Team

Union is strength.

—Idiom

As we amble gingerly to the locker room after the final buzzer, I struggle to find words for my traditional postgame speech to ease the deep pain of a demoralizing loss. Nothing comes to mind, and in the moment, I feel ill-equipped to deal with what happened in the game. Like everyone else, it seems, I am emotionally immobilized. Once we are all gathered in the locker room, I continue to search for words amid the torrent of tears flowing from many of this proud girls' varsity team. After what seems like a long, deafening silence, I realize I am focusing on the "loss" when I should be focusing on the "team" and finally speak: "Girls, this is actually a moment to celebrate. We have arrived at a pivotal and defining place in our journey together. We are, to the person, devastated, yes, but because of that, we are united in our feelings, sadness, frustration, and disappointment. This loss has brought us closer together and ignited the power of team in each of us." Slowly, if painfully, team leaders begin to speak, and eventually others follow, including some who rarely say anything in team gatherings. The flow of thoughts and outpouring of feelings is exhilarating. In the loss, the team finds new collective purpose and power.

*W*orking well with groups is essential. The principles of teamwork form the foundation for most everything we choose to do in our lives and are key ingredients for success, whether in the context of group performance or individuals working with the support of others. Any collective effort, in business

45

or otherwise, to enjoy success requires adherence to the values and principles inherent in cohesive teamwork.

Teams that work well together are efficient (often through delegation), make effective use of a broad range of talent (using the highest and best-use principle), control risk through coordinated effort, reduce individual pressure through well-defined roles, build morale through the collective mission, enhance communication (of necessity), produce greater learning opportunities for everyone, and build camaraderie and good will. Above all, groups that work well together can achieve more than what individuals operating independently can do. In other words, people working together do more and better work than a combination of their individual efforts. There are, of course, many grandiose examples of this dynamic (e.g., the odds-defying construction of the Golden Gate Bridge). But it applies at the most basic levels of group work. In the oft-quoted words of Aristotle, "The whole is greater than the sum of its parts."

In the realm of high school athletics, there is no greater power than what percolates inside the connections and bonds that are integral to team membership. Athletic teams, including both team and individual sports in high school, are the ideal vehicle to teach student-athletes about how the real world works. High school athletes are uniquely exposed to the value of team and teamwork through their entire high school athletic careers. Each athletic team operates with common purposes and goals, much like businesses and other organizations. Each athletic team has a set of values and expectations, including punctuality, loyalty, trust, work ethic, commitment, and role, again much like what student-athletes will encounter as adults. Each athletic team and its members are accountable, and everyone owns the problems of the team, as they will experience performing adult responsibilities, whether in the workplace, family settings, or other circumstances.

> *In* the realm of high school athletics, there is no greater power than what percolates inside the connections and bonds that are integral to team membership.

The essential characteristics of teamwork in sports and business are similarly elemental to success. Another high school football (and lacrosse) player, who also became a successful portfolio manager, drew a direct parallel between the dynamics of his high school team experience and the work culture he found in the finance world:

In the real world, it's almost all about teams. There aren't many jobs where you're sitting by yourself, unless you're a toll booth operator. Almost every job is reliant on team members, and you're only as strong as the weakest team member. You have to rely on other people, and you have to interact with other people, and sometimes your ass is on the line because of other people. Sometimes you're covering for other people, and sometimes other people are covering for you. There's a big connection between business and having high school teammates, because your business is a team.

Perhaps the most vibrant lesson student-athletes learn from teamwork is that accepting and embracing allocated roles is vital, and if everyone performs their role, the group will be grounded, effective, and powerful. While coaches are duty-bound to allocate roles wisely, internalizing role acceptance on an individual basis is one of the most impactful lessons a high school athlete can learn. The connection between teammates—the emotional bonding, the reliance and trust, and the power of team—is like nothing a high school student will experience. When individual members of a team—or any group, for that matter—accept their role as part of the group mission, the lessons are timeless, uplifting, and powerful. A former high school basketball player has taken those lessons to heart, not only in her work as a teacher, but within the bounds of family life as well:

> My high school teams made me feel I had a second family. I still reminisce about those days and hold dear the bonds we had. It was beautiful. When we came together on the court, we each knew our part and supported one another. It was a powerful sense of belonging. In addition to showing the beauty of group working so well together, I learned to be flexible in many areas of my life. I wasn't that way entering high school. Before, I liked to have my way. That all changed when I played high school sports. As an athlete, I had to accept my role and honor the roles of others. We each had to embrace role and do the little things that our coaches thought would make us a success. As a wife, I work as one part of a team with my husband, figuring out family logistics, including in dealing with our toddler. The same is true with my teaching job. I have learned to be flexible and go with the flow, much the same way my high school teams had to do.

High school athletes learn, too, that no individual athlete, except in the rarest of circumstances, can bring team success and that the team is more important than any individual member, a principle that transcends sports. Teams succeed when each member is on the same page about commitment to the group mission, has compassion for fellow team members, trusts that everyone will pull in the same direction, embraces individual roles, supports each team member as needed, accepts accountability in performance, and respects one another and self. When athletes experience how the collective effort transcends them as individuals and is vital to achieve group goals, they have learned a key lesson about how success in the adult world works. Each individual contribution is special, and in combination, they constitute the ticket to getting the job done, as this former soccer player learned well:

> My high school athletic experience taught me that, in a work environment, I am part of a team, too. So, when I am at work at a multidisciplinary clinic for people with mental illness, I know I'm part of a team, and each team member has a role and skill set that, in combination, produces the results we want, much like how my high school soccer team functioned. If one of us slacked off or failed to do our job, it impacted everyone.

Specific team-building activities are important components of what occurs in high school athletics. Most programs provide one or more opportunities for teams to get off campus and take part in team-oriented field trips. Those outings can vary greatly, from volunteering work in the community, ropes-climbing or similar off-site demanding physical courses, and leadership and trust-building activities. Football teams sometimes take cloistered several-day retreats at the start of the season to lay groundwork for their journey, sequestered from the rest of the world.

The benefits of team-building activities for an athletic team are many, for example: (1) acceptance of role; (2) minimizing or eliminating negative energy or influences; (3) developing leadership; (4) building team cohesion and trust; (5) improving communication; (6) demonstrating the power of collective achievement; and (7) fostering greater social acceptance and improved relationships.

Noteworthy is how the team-building experiences help coaches get to know players better and vice versa, and create powerful connections between and among teammates and between players and coaches. If one theme resonated more so than any other from the interviews for this book, it was the timeless bonds high school athletes formed with teammates and their coaches. It is as if a small part of each of their hearts took up permanent residence in the hearts of their teammates and coaches, an indelible impact to cherish. One three-sport athlete who went on to become a coach of two sports recently had a 30-year high school reunion and shared how the connections with his former teammates and coach were as vibrant as ever despite the passage of considerable time. The reuniting uplifted him.

Strong relationships are the internal fibers of successful teams and the foundation for accountability. The bonds that happen in high school sports, whether called the "sisterhood" or the "band of brothers," are what so many high school athletes take with them to the adult world. It arouses a sense of belonging and manifests power in numbers. It can be an infectious feeling that deepens commitment and spurs motivation. It arouses a shared sense to not let anyone in the group down, as each exercises the kind of discipline and loyalty that fuels collaborative work, as this former high school football player attests:

> Playing high school sports infused me with a deep responsibility to my teammates and coaches. I felt bonded to them in an unshakeable way. To make sure I stayed connected, I acted with discipline and gave full effort all the time. I didn't want to disappoint anyone. I wanted to serve my team. I learned about accountability, which, along with motivation, drove my discipline. It all applies to my adult life. Nothing happens in a vacuum in the work world. You work with partners and colleagues. You work on deals. You put yourself out there and must be accountable, which requires the same responsibility and discipline as what is expected as a teammate on a sports team. Quite literally, if you don't perform your role, the whole thing can break down.

The power of team is not limited to team sports. Individual sports like tennis, golf, and cross-country, among others, foster team-building in significant ways. A tennis coach described it this way:

> In tennis, even though it is considered an individual sport, we emphasize the team aspects. Tennis has a presumed pecking order. Nobody wants to play with anybody not as good as they are. Everyone wants to play with the better players. To build a team, however, tennis players have to spend time with one another and care about everyone else. They have to learn they must play with everyone. They learn they can work with someone as good and get better. That's the way it has to be. Otherwise, no one is going to play with you. I mean, do the math. So, the first thing for people in an individual sport to start thinking about is the team concept and to look at tennis as a collaborative activity, which helps them become less selfish and more effective leaders, skills that will come in handy in any business environment.

Professor Kevin Kniffin of Cornell conducted a study that explored whether former high school athletes make better employees than non-athletes. In concluding they do, Kniffin found that the lessons from teamwork in high school extend beyond the high school experience. In commenting on the Kniffin study, one writer noted,

> People who play sports are exposed to coaches who enforce group behaviors that don't always get emphasized in classrooms: mutual respect, trust, confidence, and teamwork. They learn to be led in a positive direction,

essentially, and to work with teammates toward a common goal. Team sports also reward group-level achievement, helping people learn how to function well within an organization. Some combination of all those skills seems to make for a better—or at least more promotable—employee.[1]

Three employers—one with four decades of trial work, a C-Suite executive in a global technology firm, and an executive with a national TV network, respectively—underscored the point in different ways:

I've been a partner in several law firms. I interviewed potential hires in each of them. We received hundreds and hundreds of resumes of very capable law students and attorneys seeking to transfer from other firms. As someone who played basketball throughout high school and college, I always looked for candidates with team sports in their histories. Invariably, they presented well in person and brought something to the table that if you're not in team sports, you are unlikely to have. That includes an understanding and respect for collaborative work, an ability to bond with and trust colleagues, and be loyal to them, have their back as it were, and how to deal with success and failure. They also bring a powerful sense of drive to work performance and are result-oriented. They want to get to the end line and know how to get there.

Employers in the technology sector, much to the surprise of people outside that market niche, consistently note when job applicants cite their athletic background in resumes, which is an acknowledgment that candidates know they derived important life lessons from their participation of sports. As an employer, I can't help but agree.

I think the major long-term impact that high school athletics have is the sense of belonging to a larger goal and being part of a larger organization. That translates to sports teams, as well as a sales organization or any company. In the entertainment workforce, I look to hire athletes, because I know they know about commitment, sacrifice, hard work, and teamwork. If I was hiring for a position and had two resumes from which to choose where the candidates were identical except one had an extensive high school or college athletic background, I would choose the athlete without question. I presume that person balanced and better able to fit into a work environment.

As noted, the specific benefits of high school sports often feed one another. An example applicable here is the interplay between self-esteem and confidence and team-building. As discussed later (in chapter 9), an athletic program that values and emphasizes affirmation of its student-athletes helps build self-esteem and confidence. As one former multisport athlete put it, high school sports "empowered" him to "earn peer respect." That, in turn, helped fuel a feeling of belonging, an inherent quality of team membership that can be crucial to strong emotional and social development. When team members feel good about themselves, the ties that bind a team become tighter and everyone's appreciation for the collective power of team more appreciated and coveted. This allows high school athletes to emerge from high school armed with the knowledge of how groups work well and how they individually are well-suited to flourish as a contributing part of the group.

Nothing in the high school experience rivals sports team magnetism and no other high school activity mirrors real-life experiences like the athletic endeavor. While academic projects can sometimes involve collaboration, and certain activities like band and dance require interactive and coordinated work, none come remotely close to the fused emotional, cognitive, and physical engagement of a sports team working tirelessly together to achieve a common goal. The high school athletic experience commands the entire athlete at all times and generates unrivaled kinship. It is at once dynamic, exhilarating, relentless, and holistic. In the catalog of high school experiences, sports teams stand out as compellingly unique.

Grade point averages, grades in specific courses, and SAT scores are hardly trifling matters. They each have an important place in building an intellectual foundation for success and an attractive resume. But in the real world, results are expected based on what we do when facing pressure in competitive situations, where intangibles make the difference in achieving long-term success in posteducational endeavors and adult relationships. High school athletes undergo a rite of competitive passage each time they show up for practice or games. It is what they do on a regular basis. Working as a thriving team member in the multidimensional high school sports environment holds tremendous long-term value that cannot be overstated. Former high school athletes bring qualities to the table in postschooling organizational situations that are unique to the athletic experience and give them an edge as leaders, businesspeople, and employees.

· 7 ·

Leadership

The most common way people give up their power is by thinking they don't have any.

—Alice Walker[1]

Once the season gets underway, I impose a study hall requirement on my varsity team. I casually dismiss their mild protests and insist that the three-day-a-week study hall schedule is in their best interests. After less than two weeks, a reticent team member who barely made the team requests a meeting with me. He asks whether I am open to a different study hall approach. I say sure, and with that opening, he pulls out a typewritten compromise the team deputized him to propose. I chuckle; it is a playful moment. It is also a precious leadership moment. I take the written offer of compromise home, tweak its terms here and there that night, and the next day present a written counteroffer to this emergent team leader in the form of a formal contract between team members and the coaching staff. He confers with the team and confirms to me that the team unanimously agrees to the counteroffer terms. Each player and member of the coaching staff signs the deal (the core of which is that study hall is reduced to one day a week, with the caveat that the schedule will increase if any team member slips academically). That year, the team receives a state award for scholastic achievement.

$\mathcal{T}$he importance of leadership is self-evident. Leadership motivates others to deliver their personal best and keeps everyone on the path to achieve group goals. Leadership infuses the group mission with commitment and resolve; models trustworthiness and consistency; inspires courage in risk-taking; and demonstrates effective communication skills, notably the power of listening. It is on the short list of the most prized skills an individual can develop.

Studies show that everyone, including student-athletes, has the capacity to lead in some manner.[2] For example, the Kellogg Foundation published research results, which included North American public and private university campuses, showing, among other things, that each student has the potential to become a leader and leadership skills can be taught. The study also showed that leadership and core values are inextricably linked.[3]

Most everyone has some qualities that leaders possess, but not everyone gets the opportunity to showcase them. Everyone can, however, develop leadership qualities and apply them in a wide range of circumstances, including in the workplace.

Opportunities for high school athletes to develop leadership skills abound, not only for team captains—"appointed" leaders—but also most every other athlete—"emergent" leaders. Appointed leaders are integral to high school sports. Every team has captains. Their leadership is expected, and they typically get the lion's share of opportunity to work with coaching staff to help steward the handling of their sport during a season. Whether or not they have natural leadership skills, they are expected to step up. It can be an awakening, but it thrusts appointed leaders into a dynamic role that can reap many benefits. Here is how one appointed leader, a former high school basketball player, handled the challenge:

> As an elected captain, I had what I would call forced leadership. But it made me learn some basic skills, including how to address a group of people and get them to listen to you and how to stand up in front of a room and talk for a bit. It is incredible how many people lack those skills, at least that's what I've found in the business world. Athletes seemed more comfortable in that role. The most direct impact of my high school sports experience is that I can stand up for myself in any meeting. I can go in there and say what needs to be said without any qualms.

Appointed leaders might take time to warm to the role. Exceptional athletes don't always make the best leaders; indeed, many times they do not, but they often get the captain nod, depending on the systems used to determine captains. This places a premium on coaches being attuned to how best to deploy elected team representatives. Appointed captains often need some hand-holding and guidance to do their jobs, including being channeled to do certain things they are best suited to handle. But regardless of how roles are allocated, the opportunity is rich with growth potential.

Emergent leaders are a different breed. They tend to have more innate and sometimes previously unexpressed leadership ability and need only opportunity to express their talent. One of the wonderful things about high school sports is that everyone can lead to some extent in the right circumstance if they choose, especially when coaches encourage them. Here coaches can parse how best to use emergent leaders in tailored circumstances. At the high school level, all emergent leaders typically need is a dose of positive influence to break out to lead. It is easily done. For example, as in any classroom, a coach can call on players to demonstrate skills in practice or, even more significantly, run an entire drill for the team. A more prominent opportunity is having a player or group of players design and run a practice.

Setting boundaries between appointed and emergent is not always easy. The athletic experience can be too fluid and encompassing to erect artificial barriers to define leadership roles. For example, dealing with game officials, acting as team ambassadors, or bringing problems or disputes to the coaching staff are well-suited for appointed leaders. On the other hand, leadership displayed in other contexts defies limitations, for example, leading by the example of a dedicated work ethic, sound nutritional habits, stellar academic performance, or other model behavior. These later instances are not conducive to discrete role definition and are naturally within the domain of any team member.

Coaches sometimes provide their leaders with lists of what, to their way of thinking, constitutes positive and negative leadership. For example, the most obvious is modeling team-first behavior. Others might include being teacher-oriented instead of authoritative, yielding control instead of insisting on having it, pursuing the team vision rather than worrying about short-term results, valuing consensus or group-based decision-making to the exclusion of doing whatever they want or is best for them, and looking to learn from errors in contrast to blaming others or getting frustrated with teammates. Motivational speaker Jim Rohn captured the traits of leadership in poetic terms: "The challenge of leadership is to be strong, but not rude; be kind, but not weak; be bold, but not bully; be thoughtful, but not lazy; be humble, but not timid; be proud, but not arrogant; have humor, but without folly."[4]

Sometimes it is merely a matter of athletes seizing learning opportunities that fall at their feet, as happened to this former basketball player:

> High school basketball made me comfortable in a leadership role, which I never anticipated would happen. On the job, as an adult, I thrust myself into a take-charge role because I feel I am either on the bus or off. There is no in-between for me. I want to help direct as much as I can, and I became comfortable doing that in high school. Even though I wasn't a team captain, I knew I'd proven to myself that I could take on a leadership role and motivate people that way. I've been praised for speaking up and helping others get involved. I have been told that I am willing to solve

problems and even am bold sometimes. I appreciate that so much. Looking back, high school hoops had a big role in getting me primed for being able to do that.

Leading is not easy. It can be tough getting people to listen and work together to benefit the team or group as a whole. Coaches can sometimes find that their attempts to lead fall on deaf ears. There can come a time during the season where head coaches tire of their own voices. When that happens, they can be assured others have tired of them as well. To model leadership, it is important to recognize the most effective channels of guidance and, like any life situation, identify who is best able to handle leadership challenges in specific situations. Sometimes it is the head coach. Sometimes it is an assistant. And sometimes it is one of the athletes. This is an important lesson for student-athletes. They need to understand that team leaders, especially captains, have more in common with their teammates and often, as a result, have an inside track to impact them favorably. The realization that leadership can and often should be delegated or transmitted below the chain of command is an important educational moment, especially when the coaching staff reaffirms that underlying principle.

Leadership in athletic programs, as elsewhere, can be expressed in many ways in accordance with personal style. High school athletic leaders need not fit a model of leadership. There is no one-size-fits-all exemplar for leadership or right or wrong way to lead. Most important is that athletes understand if they want to lead, they should be themselves and be positive. Individual leadership styles, especially at this stage of emotional development, are what should be encouraged. Of course, some lead with the power of words and presence. Others lead by how they conduct themselves, "by example," as we say, like this former swimmer, whose high school leadership role has served him well in business management as an adult:

> My leadership experience in high school was about putting my best foot forward for the team. I feel like high school made me into a good leader and teammate, and I feel like those are good, important pieces of who I am post-athletics. While I led more by example than vocal, I wasn't afraid to tell someone something. I remember one time our goal was to win the state championship for high school, and our team morale wasn't really where we needed it to be. I called a team meeting and asked the coaches not to be present. I wanted the team to know this was coming from me and the other two captains, and was important to us. I wanted to inspire everyone to step up as best they could. I think when you hear something from your coaches it is important, but when you hear it from your teammates, it goes a bit further. I now manage the same way, trying to set clear goals and set up staff for success to grow their careers. I spend time trying

to guide them in the right direction and give them room to make mistakes and ask questions. I can't do the work for them, but I can train them to execute the right way.

Letting athletes know they have value in a leadership role is empowering. The more coaches believe in them, the more student-athletes will believe in themselves. The more leadership is spread among the team, the greater the investment each athlete has in the team and the outcome of its efforts. On a specific skill basis, high school athletic programs provide a rich collection of skills available to student-athletes who assume leadership roles. Any one of them is useful and more than one, in combination, a boon: displaying enhanced maturity; exhibiting role model skills; feeling comfort being an ambassador to the public; commanding and giving respect; exercising mental toughness when facing pressure; being a team-first performer; displaying positivity, loyalty, and empathy; maintaining consistency in adhering to applicable values; implementing effective communication skills; and having a tendency to see the big picture.

Leadership arms student-athletes with a toolbox equipped with effective strategies and abilities to serve them for a long time.

Leadership arms student-athletes with a toolbox equipped with effective strategies and abilities to serve them for a long time. Strong leadership skills will prepare affected student-athletes for most anything that will drop in front of them down the road. As studies have shown, in business, government, and other professional cultures, people tend to expect former student-athletes to demonstrate greater leadership, confidence, and self-respect than others who have no or little athletic background. High school athletes, especially team leaders, often know how to motivate others, provide feedback to allow others to succeed, and create situations where others can do their jobs well.[5] One former two-sport high school athlete found a leadership groove in the roles he played for his teams, which holds him in good stead in the work he does with youth today:

> I certainly learned to be vocal in team settings, address crowds, and take on leadership and decision-making roles thanks to high school sports. Those years, on those teams, were my first real opportunities to practice those skills in meaningful ways. That has stayed with me, especially the value of teaching youth through leadership.

Kevin Kniffin, who, as noted, ran a study at Cornell University to explore whether former high school athletes make better employees than non-athletes, had this to say after the release of the study results:

> One of the reasons that we propose there's a positive spillover of team-oriented traits and behaviors to other domains of life and work is that players—in youth sports, especially—are exposed to role models—adult coaches, specifically—who tend to be passionate about their leadership of their respective teams. . . . Something very special happens on scholastic playing fields and tracks and basketball courts. Student-athletes, whether or not they are captains or leaders of their teams, are exposed to leaders in an environment that rewards transformational leadership. The focus in youth sports is on prosocial traits: respect, trust, and confidence. That experience spills over wherever their adult lives take them.[6]

The experience of a high school water polo player illustrates the point:

> In my senior year in high school, I became comfortable as a team leader of the water polo team, which I built on throughout the years. Now, far removed from high school days, my job as a leader, especially as we scale and I gain more responsibility, is to set up a system that allows for accountability and performance. I need to empower my people to do their job. That is setting a vision, holding them accountable, making sure they know what they're doing every day, helping them when they're down, pushing them when things are a little too soft, and being their coach. At the end of the day, my goals are dependent on how they perform. It's the same with a coach, the same I experienced in high school.

Coaches can teach their athletes that leadership is a process of influence designed to achieve purposeful results. It requires initiative, awareness, and an appreciation for the strengths and limitations of teammates, as well as understanding of personal values. It represents a commitment to perpetual learning.

There are good leaders and not-so-good leaders in the larger world. The high school athletic leader is primed to be the former, owing in the main to the context in which their leadership skills are nurtured. While not all coaches are natural leaders, they can help their athletes learn the ropes of leadership. High school sports are breeding grounds for leadership. Student-athletes who enjoy leadership experience emerge better and more grounded people, poised to extend their leadership influence after schooling based on a value system calculated to inject positive impact wherever they go. Increasingly, we need more people among us with those skills and inclinations, and high school sports present the ideal environment to develop that vital human resource.

· 8 ·

Citizenship and Community

For a community to be whole and healthy, it must be based on people's love and concern for each other.

—Millard Fuller, Habitat for Humanity founder[1]

Before we embark on a three-hour journey for an overnight tournament, I remind the team what I wrote a few days earlier: They are school ambassadors whenever in public, a role more pronounced when we visit a different community, especially a small town, like where we are headed. I tell them they will be "on" every moment of the trip and need to take model behavior to new heights. We want to leave the local community with the impression that a band of saints passed through town draped in athletic gear. After we return from the tournament, I receive an e-mail from the host school, not only complimenting us on our competitive showing, but also exclaiming how well behaved the team was, how polite and deferential each player was to everyone, and how they couldn't ask for a better group of kids to participate in their annual tournament. I read the e-mail to the team at the next practice, offer my commentary, and tell them how proud I am of them. A few players speak, but one comment resonates: "Coach, after we arrived the first day, the team met and discussed that we should treat everyone there like we would want them to treat us and that, if we did that, we would show respect and get invited back."

$\mathcal{U}$pholding the highest standards of civility, respect, and understanding of others is a baseline for public behavior. This is especially so in our increasingly diverse and contentious global world. We want our youth to have a sense of

59

community, understand and embrace the world outside theirs, honor our communal existence, have a respectful attitude toward others, and bask in the beauty and benefits of multiculturalism. The more they experience other communities, the more familiar they will become with the differences among us and more comfortable and accepting of different cultures and ways of life, including the sometimes-alienating boundaries of social and cultural stratification at schools. The interactive part of exposure to other communities helps communication skills as well.

Fundamentally, high school sports foster a fulfilling sense of belonging that both supplies the glue to bind members of a community and gives each community member a sense of purpose and meaning. Down deep, most of us want to contribute to the greater good, to know we can help others in a way that transcends ourselves, a value high school sports can help nurture. High school athletes have a bird's-eye view of what it means to belong to a community. At the local school level, most every day, they experience the intricacy of community, a sense of inclusion that yields purpose, as high school sports foster community awareness within the high school milieu. Student-athletes not only enjoy a distinct identity on campus, but also function regularly as part of an active collaboration among school administrators, coaches, team managers, and parents as members of a small and thriving community within the larger community.

Being a good citizen does not automatically follow from athletic participation. Citizenship is a responsibility that values the common good, serves the community well, and honors rules. Developing good citizen-athletes occurs within the ambit of sports relationships, for example, between athlete and athlete, athlete and team, athlete and coach, in the context of the community. Connecting athletes to the community is essential to any athletic program. The community is part of local high school sports teams, and the role of the community should be highlighted throughout the school year and with each sports program.

Because they are the most public of any feature of the high school experience, high school athletic programs are the keepers of school culture and values.

Among other things, competition teaches student-athletes about the efficacy and necessity of rules, both in terms of honoring the many of them that govern their sport and handling the repercussions that come with not following them. In a rule-based athletic environment, they get to compete within the bigger picture of how rules are applied on a constant basis, in practice and acutely in game situations, and provide the stability and order essential to the athletic experience. Learning how that works is groundwork for how things work in the real world, where the stakes are much higher. As part of that experience, student-athletes learn to respect institutions and others' talents and abilities. Hopefully, the experience will also provide the ability to rationally recognize the relative importance of events in their lives and make sound judgments based on those priorities. Athletics can put things in perspective in a value-based program.

High school athletes are in a unique position to develop an appreciation for the world outside of campus. Because they are the most public of any feature of the high school experience, high school athletic programs are the keepers of school culture and values. Sports competition bridges school and the community. More than anyone else, student-athletes are the ambassadors of their high school. Whether embarking on a fundraising mission, performing community service, participating in an athletic field trip, competing in front of home crowds, or traveling to other communities to compete as a team, student-athletes are called on regularly to be the face of the school. It gives them the opportunity to display behavior that reflects on the school and broadens their sense of community.

While high school sports don't stand alone in providing these opportunities for students, they do provide the most conspicuous and pervasive exposure to the community. Student-athletes are the first-tier public ambassadors for their schools. In so many ways, the chance to be out front in the community is a gift student-athletes should be encouraged to cherish. It is an experience central to high school sports programs and, with rare exception, cannot be replicated in traditional classrooms, as this former student-athlete reaffirmed:

> Not to deride science, math, or any other class, but high school athletic programs are in the community, and we student-athletes were the collective representatives of the values of the schools. We stood for the school every day, especially when on the road. We were fortunate to have the opportunity to have that role in the community.

The community aspect of high school athletes implicates the nature of the value system schools elect to embrace. The following is how one coach tackled the challenge:

> Our high school athletes were expected to show uncompromising respect for others and represent themselves in the most positive way possible. We were expected to consistently ask ourselves these questions: How well do

you represent yourself? How well do you represent your teammates, your high school, and your community? How well do you represent your parents? Your family? Those were the overriding considerations for our high school program.

In August 2017, the National Federation of State High School Associations (NFHS) posted an article by Bob Gardner entitled "High School Activities Bring Communities Together." The following excerpts speak volumes:

> Attending high school sporting events teaches important life lessons, too.
> Among them, it teaches that we can live in different communities, come from different backgrounds, faiths, and cultures, cheer for different teams, and still have a common bond.
> That's why attending the activities across the country this fall is so important. It's not only an opportunity to cheer for your hometown team, it is also an opportunity to celebrate our commonality. And that's something our country needs right now.
> The bond we share is mutually supporting the teenagers in our respective communities. We applaud their persistence, tenacity, preparation, and hard work, regardless of the color of the uniform they wear. We acknowledge that education-based high school sports are enhancing their lives, and ours, in ways that few other activities could. And we agree that, regardless of what side of the field we sit on, attending a high school sporting event is an uplifting, enriching, family friendly experience for all of us.
> Many of the high schools in the United States lie at the heart of the communities they serve. They not only are educating our next generation of leaders, they also are a place where we congregate, where people from every corner of town and all walks of life come together as one. And at no time is this unity more evident than during a high school athletic event.[2]

The words of former United Nations secretary-general Kofi Annan sounded a similar note on a much larger stage:

> Sport is a universal language. At its best it can bring people together, no matter what their origin, background, religious beliefs, or economic status. And when young people participate in sports or have access to physical education, they can experience real exhilaration, even as they learn the ideals of teamwork and tolerance. That is why the United Nations is turning more and more to the world of sport for help in our work for peace and our efforts to achieve the Millennium Development Goals.[3]

High school athletics have vast potential to introduce their participants to communities beyond their own, both in terms of exposure to other schools from different demographic bases, as well as road games and tournaments that bring them into communities outside their normal life patterns. Both happen regularly within the course of an athletic year. When they do, student-athletes, especially with appropriate guidance and mentoring, get the chance to see beyond the narrow contours of their worlds and put their life in perspective in the larger community and world, as this conscientious, multisport high school athlete was able to do:

> High school sports offered a chance to interact with individuals and communities that are widely diverse. It helped break down walls, build bridges, and challenge stereotypes. It was the first time I began to evaluate my place in the world and how I fit into historical formations. It also helped teach the value of every human by being on a team where each person, no matter how small the role, is invaluable to success.

The benefit this produces cannot be understated. To find early in life a sense of belonging to a larger composition—a basic human need—and that everyone matters to one another is a blessing. We live in an era when this sense of connection is needed more than ever. While expressing this somewhat tongue-in-cheek, a former high school basketball player, who has enjoyed a long professional career as an attorney, stressed the real-life impact of enjoying a sense of community in high school:

> High school sports broadened my horizons. I was from a predominantly white suburban school, and by virtue of basketball, I spent a lot of time in socioeconomically different neighborhoods and with a lot of my closest friends to this day, who are African Americans, to the point where 35 years later they still call me "White Shadow" because I was the one white kid at the local community center. The experience created an abiding sense of belonging to a larger world, which carried over to the workforce after schooling.

Research shows that, in general, the longer youth play sports, the greater attachment they have to their communities and more involved they are in community activities throughout a lifetime. It also shows that youth who participate in sports activities in high school are more likely than nonparticipants to donate money to charity, engage in regular volunteering, vote, and feel comfortable speaking in a public setting.[4]

Athletics also promote school pride, which is on display when the community comes together for athletic contests. This can take various forms, for instance, prep rallies, homecoming events, and senior nights, and is commonly expressed through spirit-wear apparel that promotes the school or a specific team. The resulting pride creates meaningful and deep bonds between and among athletes, the school, and the local community that span a lifetime.

High school athletics contribute to communities in another way: Athletes are less prone to antisocial behavior. A 2015 report in the *Journal of Adolescent Health*, "High School Sports Involvement Diminishes the Association between Childhood Conduct Disorder and Adult Antisocial Behavior," indicated that high school athletics help disrupt antisocial behavior that has roots in childhood and adolescence. Thus, the more high school athletes are exposed to the community through athletics, the more aligned their behavior with social expectations and the better citizens they become.[5]

Consider these compelling comments about community from a high school coach whose sports programs place community at the top of important values he wants his high school athletes to acquire:

> Our basketball program runs on rules that foster a sense of inclusion for each athlete and a family atmosphere, so kids can be themselves. We look beyond the student-athlete to take a look at the whole person and see where they fit in the outside community. We give them the chance to belong to something. We tell them, "When you put on this uniform, you have to be a good citizen first, a good person in or out of the uniform." We help them as best we are able, but being a good person is on them. We will go the extra mile, but they have to meet us halfway. I think kids appreciate that. We are most proud when we see our athletes become good citizens. We stress to them that younger kids see them walking around the school and come to see you play. You have a responsibility to them wholly apart from a good athletic show. My greatest pride is seeing them embrace that responsibility to the community.
>
> We set—and enforce—community standards. For example, we were playing a football game against a rival school. It was muddy, and many pileups and minor scuffles were taking place. I called timeout and told the team, "If anybody else fights on the field, I'm taking you off the field. Period. You're not going to embarrass the school." So, a couple of plays later, there is a fight, and we pulled the team off the field and forfeited a game we were about to win. Afterward, we had a long discussion. I told them, "You can't play on this team not understanding who you represent. You're representing the community, your parents, and your high school. You may not wear this uniform and represent this high school the way you did, especially getting a warning from me. This is going to stop!" And it did.

The concept of sports as a means to promote social capital—and help build networked communities—is not new. It is centuries old. More recently, a 2007 study performed in Canada found a positive correlation between sports participants and lifetime volunteerism. It also found that sports inherently help children socialize and form relationships. The study, conducted by researchers from the University of Ottawa and the University of Toronto, further found that older youth involved in sports scored high on the social capital index and were more likely to continue being active in their communities and volunteer throughout their life span.[6]

If nothing else comes out of a high school athletic program but a procession of good, community-minded citizens, schools have done a fabulous job and made admirable contributions to local communities, the nation, and beyond. They have introduced people to the world who are respectful, have compassion for others, understand we each exist in a much larger community of people, and are committed to making the world a better place. That is no small achievement.

· 9 ·

Self-Esteem and Confidence

You are very powerful, provided you know how powerful you are.

—Yogi Bhajan, spiritual teacher and yogi[1]

One of my basketball players is voted best male athlete of the year at the high school and has taken the podium at the annual athletic banquet to give an acceptance speech. At one point, he gives me the obligatory thanks but then proceeds to tell a story about our first personal interaction (of which I have no memory). It was the summer between his sophomore and junior years, a mere several weeks after I got the job as varsity head coach. We were standing on the sidelines in the gym watching other players on the floor when I mentioned in passing that I was chagrined I would lose him and a few others to graduation after the upcoming season. He said, "But I'm only a junior, coach." In response, I said, "Really? Well, son, you just made my day." He proceeds to explain to the assemblage of parents, athletes, coaches, teachers, and administrative personnel that this side comment, which I had forgotten, "changed my life." For the first time since entering high school, after suffering virtually no recognition or encouragement as a basketball player, he felt affirmed and believed in, and his confidence soared. The next two years, he led the team in scoring and was team MVP and league player of the year his senior year. His comment at the banquet deeply moved me, but more importantly, it served as a poignant reminder of the impact coaches can have on the self-esteem and self-worth of their athletes.

$\mathcal{S}$elf-esteem—how we value and believe in ourselves—pervades virtually everything we do. It affects how we form relationships, trust our instincts, perform on the job, address conflict, inspire and mentor others, and chart our life paths. While strong self-esteem doesn't guarantee success and while confidence and self-esteem don't always go hand in hand, when it's strong, self-esteem gives us purpose and resolve. And while self-esteem may sometimes be the product of good performance rather than the reverse, however you slice it, it deserves special attention. This much is clear: High self-esteem correlates with happiness. It seems beyond challenge that we should constantly strive to affirm one another and create environments, whether social, business, academic, recreational, or competitive, that help us feel good about ourselves.

High school athletics are flush with opportunities for coaches, parents, and school administrators to build self-esteem in student-athletes. As the opening scenario shows, coaches sometimes forget how easily they can impact the self-worth of the youth they mentor. The words of a coach are powerful tools. Beyond express commentary, coaches influence how student-athletes see themselves through nonverbal communication, including body language, decision-making, and conduct. In response to my question about coaching styles in different eras, the late John Wooden told me and my sons that he would not coach any differently today than he did in his time because, as he put it, "Kids still need two basic things: discipline and love."

$\mathcal{H}$igh school athletics are flush with opportunities for coaches, parents, and school administrators to build self-esteem in student-athletes.

An athletic director with more than 40 years' coaching experience said the following about the interplay of confidence, belief, and love:

> Confidence is the big thing. You have to believe in yourself. As you get older, to do anything in life, you have to believe in yourself. I want every kid who's put on that uniform for me to feel special, and one way to feel special is to express love for one another, through moments that are challenging. Sometimes we need love the most when we deserve it the least. Sometimes we need to show there are other things that make us special and we are part of a team, even though we're not starting, we have a role, giving water to the players coming off the floor or clapping hands for the defense. No matter what it is, everyone is made to feel a big part of this

team. It's important that we create a family and we understand this is a time of innocence.

Among the vast array of impacts high school sports have on the development of student-athletes, self-esteem and confidence are probably the most universal. A close second to teammate bonding as a prevalent theme in the interviews for this book was how much high school sports improved self-image and confidence. Virtually everyone interviewed shared excitement about how their athletic experience grounded them personally and empowered them to succeed after high school. The following is a small sampling of how former high school athletes described that experience for themselves and how one parent described the experience of her daughter:

You start with every experience is personal. Everybody has a story, a life story. What I got out of high school basketball was self-esteem. It made me feel wanted and needed. It saved me.

My daughter obtained 95 percent of her confidence from high school sports. The more she improved as an athlete, the more confidence she had in high school. Because of sports, she ran for and was elected president of her freshman and sophomore classes, and had the courage to sing in an acapella group. Basketball gave her comfort to feel good about herself, which has paid dividends in her early adult life, inspiring her to undertake leadership roles when appropriate and knowing the differences in group roles in different situations.

Coach gave us all confidence. We were just a bunch of guys from Central Valley, and coach created an atmosphere where we just went out and had fun. He was very respectful and made us be respectful to one another. He helped us believe in ourselves. To this day, I carry that genuine feeling with me, and I try to transfer it to the kids I coach and teach. My focus is always to put them in positions to be successful and let them know I have confidence in them.

In high school, owing to football, my self-esteem improved dramatically. And when I started to excel in football, it really closed a loop for me in terms of how I saw myself, and that was powerful for me.

Growing up in an age when women's sports in high school were in their formative years, I was surrounded by women who said, "Of course you can do that! Yes, you can do that! Look what I achieved," and they were life-changing mantras for me. They made me believe I could set the world ablaze. I couldn't always, of course, and that was disappointing, but from high school I had that in me so I always found a way to make it happen.

I feel that the concentration of power I have now is greater because of my involvement in high school athletics. I have a more dialed-in focus on everything I do because of the high-intensity physical activity in high school, whether I am engaged with problem-solving on the job or even reading a book. My perseverance can be intense, much like how I played soccer in high school. "I know I can do this. I can get to the top of that mountain." Whatever it is, I know I can do it. I am always trying to prove myself to myself. I consistently have that drive.

Entering high school, I was an insecure kid, which changed because of high school sports. It gave me a new and permanent confidence, thanks in no small part to my coach, who helped me mature and accomplish so much. I don't remember thinking, "That English teacher really helped my confidence with that grade I got." My basketball coach was a different matter.

There can a flip side to this, of course. Sometimes the identity as an athlete can extend too far. Here is a former multisport athlete who wrapped his identity in athletics a little too tightly:

Playing high school sports was the foundation for my personal identity. There were other aspects of myself—ethnicity, appearance, and musical interests, etc.—that played a role, but at the core I saw myself as an athlete. In hindsight, this wasn't the healthiest situation. It caused my self-esteem and confidence to waver with sport outcomes as I tried constantly to be viewed as the best athlete. It also made transition in college more difficult when, because of injury after my freshman year, I was no longer playing basketball for my school and I had to relearn who I was and ground myself with a new identity and passion. But I figured it out.

Each illustration underscores the power of the sports medium. Each also underscores the importance of adult guidance along the way to ensure a balance in how student-athletes see themselves. Student-athletes need to see themselves as capable on multiple fronts. Sports in high school, in terms of personal development, are mainly a means, not an end. They are, at the most celebrated level, a vehicle to not only empower the student-athlete as a competitive athlete, but also help them become a whole person. The adult and peer support systems available at the high school level are vital assets for the student-athlete.

Self-esteem is constantly on the line for the student-athlete, and if adults keep affirmation constantly on their radar, the impact will be positive and lasting. The more an athlete believes in themselves as inherently important and valuable, the harder they tend to work and the more effort they tend to devote. The increased time and effort reflects the positivity they feel about themselves. Student-athletes who believe in themselves develop standards for giving their best that exalt the importance of preparation. They develop grit, which drives them to their goals with focus and perseverance, as they begin to see accomplishment as a marathon process and know success means they must stay the course. Goal achievement in that environment generates a powerful sense of what can be achieved.

It is no wonder, therefore, studies show that student-athletes demonstrate a higher level of self-confidence than non-athletes, which persists well past graduation, and that competitive sports minimize the risks of low social acceptance and produce positive traits that extend far beyond high school.[2] Studies also show that high school athletes develop self-control, character, independence, perseverance, and discipline (not to mention improved psychological function), and as a result, are more likely than non-athletes to move on to postsecondary education and, later, have higher employment rates, enjoy greater income, and ascend to high-status careers. Moreover, studies confirm that numerous CEOs and other members of management participated in scholastic sports.[3]

The Kniffin study recommended that employers include questions about participation in youth sports in job interviews.[4] Consider the comments of Ken Marschner, while executive director of UBS: "We try to recruit people that can work in a team environment, are competitive and driven, and it is not a pre-requisite, but many athletes have those traits."[5] Steve Reinemund, former chairman and CEO of PepsiCo, has stated, "In my 30 years in the business world, I have found that what an athlete brings to the workplace is discipline, teamwork, a drive for success, the desire to be held accountable, and a willingness to have their performance measured."[6]

High school students navigate through a sensitive and fragile time of life, and crave positive recognition, probably more so than at any other time of their lives. There may be no more debilitating impairment to personal growth than feeling unworthy or substandard. Sports are unique in that they provide *daily* opportunities for student-athletes to enjoy the benefits of uplifting attention, especially in how they provide rapid-fire moments for athletes to experience themselves, their internal selves, in the context of athletic activities. Like no other activity, sports, and at bottom all play, feeds the full panoply of our being—cognitive, physical, and emotional—and for that reason, they are wonderful sources to develop strong internal composition in life-affirming ways. In high school, the multidimensional self-teaching aspect of sports overflows with ways to learn about the inner self and, in the process, become validated and infused with self-worth, which is unmatched by any other high school educational experience.

The modern-day transformation from traditional to progressive education provides an even richer environment for that personal growth to flourish through high school sports. Progressive education embraces principles that similarly are embedded in valued-based high school sports programs, for example, that education is life, not preparation for it, that the community extends the classroom and is not a distinct entity, that effective teachers facilitate learning and don't merely impart information, that educational programs are guided by missions, philosophies, and goals, and are not top-down administrative mandates housed in external criteria, and that knowledge occurs through real-time engagement in activities and not the passive infusion of lectures.

A high school tennis coach made a similar observation:

> As a high school coach of many years, I have found that high school sports give kids an opportunity wholly distinct from the classroom. Student-athletes have more freedom to be themselves, grow at exponential rates, and express themselves in different ways instead of fitting into classroom rules and linear or standardized behavior. One of the great things is watching them grow up, change, and begin to become something resembling a full person. There's still much growth to happen, of course, but the changes that sports at this level nurture are enormous. When it happens, it's wonderful to see. I love seeing the kids grow so expansively.

The world today has become exceedingly complex. It pounds us with information and misinformation at dazzling and dizzying rates, which can confuse, overwhelm, and unsettle at times. The environment today coughs up too many reasons to be unhappy and lack drive. One antidote is the capacity to feel good about ourselves, moving through life with buoyancy. High school sports are a superior tool for infusing our youth with the confidence and feel-good self-perception that will allow them to manage pressure, overcome distractions, and cut through the dark and perplexing moments of life with budding resolve.

The Pursuit of Consistency in Excellence

Excellence is doing ordinary things extraordinarily well.

—John Gardner, Common Cause founder[1]

As a high school football player, Dante displays a wide range of talent, except he suffers from inconsistency in performance, sometimes a wide range. Mindful of his potential and expressed commitment to the game, coach sits down with him to review his workout habits outside of team activities and sees they reflect the inconsistency he exhibits in games and sometimes in practices. They discuss habits, routines, goals, and values, and the challenge and difficulty of achieving consistency in performance and the pursuit of excellence. Coach tells him he has to decide where high school football ranks on his list of life priorities. To be more consistent in game situations, if that is important to him, he must be more consistent in his preparation regimes. In response, with coaching staff help, he develops routines that reflect long-term focus and commitment. Step by step, sometimes in barely discernible increments, his performance becomes more consistent and his confidence rises. By his senior year, he has become a consistent contributor because he is reliable and poised in pressure situations.

Consistency is a life thread to weave through everything we do. It allows us to achieve excellence in performance through the power of incremental steps. It grounds us, fosters meaningful change in our lives, creates momentum, and, in the process, produces confidence. It also allows us to establish standards for measuring performance and accountability. Because consistency aligns our values, words, and behavior, it also enhances reputation. People can trust what to expect from us. Socrates had a bead on this: "The way to gain a good reputation is to endeavor to be what you desire to appear."[2]

In the world marketplace, consistency brings repeat business from satisfied consumers and generates referrals and recommendations. Most any business of any scale can achieve its goals with consistency in strategy, planning, and execution. In the workplace, consistent performance gives others the confidence and trust that we are reliable and can get the job done day in and day out. Whether running a business or a marathon, cultivating personal relationships, raising children, getting and staying healthy and fit, or nurturing personal growth and character, consistency is essential.

Consistency in excellence is a formidable and worthy challenge in high school athletics. Sterling athletic performance on any given day is not uncommon. Most athletic teams and athletes can spring a great performance or two. What drives the athletic mission each year, however, is generating the same level of performance on a consistent basis, the pinnacle of athletic achievement. It can be a steep curve, as one coach pointed out:

> Coaches have to constantly look for ways to bring out the best in their athletes, and sometimes they can't find it. How to connect effort to results is not always easy. Discovering the inner resources of players is essential and sometimes takes time. It is a journey. There must be a steady drumbeat of learning and progress, leading to the pursuit of constant excellence. There is no escaping the pathway; there are no shortcuts or crash courses. It is all in the good habits of hard and focused work.

In high school sports culture, keen competition in practice inherently pushes toward excellence in performance standards. Coaches typically try to make practice more challenging than what games command. Competition in practice is designed to make players better by not only working on important aspects of the sport and getting prepared for games, but also having each athlete commit to making teammates better by challenging them as much as they are able. It is a daily sports ritual. A common coaching technique, at the start of practice, is to urge team members to endeavor to emerge from practice a better player than they entered and help their teammates do the same. That doesn't mean competing to win or beating teammates at something. It means competing to push one another to fulfill potential, regardless of the measured result. It is an attitude that relegates the status of winners and losers to a lower rung on the ladder in favor of developing enhanced competitors. When teammates work hard to make teammates better, they push the envelope of potential and help one another achieve consistency of excellence. It sometimes comes down to having consistent program standards that guide how the team and its athletes progress. Going through the motions of drills is a good baseline, but it's hardly sufficient to create sound habits. Players must understand what is expected of them and know what is needed to consistently toe the line of quality in performance. The march toward excellence can be unyielding, as this multisport athlete recognized:

> When I look back, I always think of coaches who had standards. They used the concept of team to raise the bar of what they expected of us and push us. We couldn't let teammates down. I'm grateful for coaches who not only believed in me, but also put me in situations that demanded great effort.

In the trenches, consistency in excellence in athletics requires, foremost, attention to detail. The late coach John Wooden often talked about the importance of the little things, from the precise way to lace up basketball shoes to the specifics of how to hold the basketball before executing a pass. As he liked to say, "Little things make big things happen."[3] Coaches endeavor to teach detailed elements of the skills their sport requires. The collective body of details that skill sets implicate in high school sports is virtually unquantifiable. Among many others, to illustrate, they include such things as the following: the proper technique for boxing out an offensive player when vying for a defensive rebound; the execution of the chip pass in soccer; how to engage the muscles of the lower body to generate power in a volley in tennis; the method for catching, placing, and holding the football for the kicker attempting a field goal; the proper way to lower the hips when a wrestler seeks a takedown; the execution of the last three steps in the high jump; how to exchange the baton in a track relay; and the deft use of the long pole when attempting a shot on goal in lacrosse.

*P*recision in execution and economy of movement are what produce the best results and introduce standards of performance to student-athletes that can last a lifetime.

There is a visualization and intensity of focus and discipline required to master the little things to make a difference, and student-athletes enjoy a wealth of opportunity to experience what it takes. A lacrosse goalie described for me how he used a tennis ball machine that shot 500 balls at a clip at him at angles he set up and speeds that rival a fastball in baseball to refine his ability to protect the goal. He was incrementally building muscle memory. Shots on goal in lacrosse sometimes top 100 miles per hour, and he wanted to improve his ability to move in a split second when facing an offensive attack. He now draws on that experience in business:

> It taught me that achieving something is the compilation of many small moments. It's like you can't leap and bound to get through things. It's stutter stepping. There are so many tiny, tiny, little things, which if you continue the pattern, eventually the momentum starts to pick up and you land where you want to be.

The underlying lesson is that shortcuts don't cut it. Precision in execution and economy of movement are what produce the best results and introduce standards of performance to student-athletes that can last a lifetime. A regular emphasis on adhering to the small details and skill precision is calculated to deliver top-flight performance and value. Here is an inspirational tale illustrating that principle from a former high school swimmer functioning at a top competitive level, which helped fortify him for his management work later in life:

> Swimming, in some respects, is more science than art. What's interesting to me is the precision of each increment. As a senior in high school, I had offers to go to a few different colleges. I chose Michigan. The coach at that time was Bob Bowman, Michael Phelps's coach. So, I crossed over with Michael when I was there. I like to tell my students a story about Michael, when Coach Bowman one day got us out of the pool and talked about streamline, when you come up to the wall to make a turn in a precise manner. Coach stressed the difference of putting your thumb here rather than there to increase aerodynamics, an imperceptible difference to the eye, and we all made that minute change that day. Two months later, Michael won his eight gold medals, including a race he won by .01 second on a great touch finish. Maybe that day in practice made the difference, that very small but huge detail. Excellence is the product of attention to detail, which can be minute. In the real world, I apply application of those details to my job and most anything I do. You never know when that little extra disciplined-effort is going to make a difference.

Excellence requires discipline, commitment, unwavering focus, and task-concentration. The combination brings an intensity that is hard to replicate outside of sports. It can be all-consuming, even obsessively so. Not every program is or can be the same when it comes to intensity of work regimes and the goals that are at stake. That doesn't mean, however, we can't each learn from how the most successful get it done. When high school athletes learn what it takes to ring the proverbial bell, it allows them to dial in performance in a powerful way, as this former basketball player learned in working with one the greatest hoopsters of all time:

High school sports led me to an epiphany, what I call a "holy shit" moment. I learned what it takes to produce excellence at all times. We had a player in high school, known now around the world, who worked harder than anyone I ever saw in any discipline, and I've been around a lot of successful people. In high school, being exposed to that kind of intensity impacted me forever in a huge way.

The road to repeated excellence in athletics implicates a sense of responsibility to others that sets sports in high school apart from the classroom. High school athletes don't operate in isolation or a vacuum. They perform within the sphere of a connected small community, and most understand that how they perform, on many levels, impacts others in various ways. It is a unique responsibility and sense of purpose. A multisport athlete described what this meant to him:

> High school sports taught me responsibility in execution. I wasn't only responsible to myself, but also to teammates and parents, the school, friends who came to watch you play, and the coaching staff. That is a large community of people who believe in you and trust you. To give anything but what it takes to deliver excellence in performance is disrespectful of the people who have put so much belief in you. I never wanted to waste anything. I wanted to show up all the time and be as good as possible. I realized that, if I always gave 100 percent, everything would come out better, even if we didn't get the precise result we wanted. Consistency of effort at the highest level is the ultimate goal in performance, a standard that is valuable for anything I will face in life.

These qualities distill to sound and consistent good habits, and the ability to stay on task no matter what the challenge or distraction. Most student-athletes are tested every day. While some sports are more vigorous than others—football can push the boundaries of tolerance and capacity more than most—each high school sport challenges its athletes to stay focused on the task at hand and be diligent about developing workable routines and sound habits. One high school football player viewed the rigor of his experience as groundwork for adulthood:

> We did killer sprints every day, and each week they got considerably harder. It was like climbing a mountain that had no peak. And then there was coming to practice every day in the summer when all your friends are goofing off, going to the beach; that's tough. I think the rigor of high school football enabled me, many years later, to get up at 5:00 a.m. to catch the train every day when I needed to be at work, or be the first one on the desk, or to stay the late hours or whatever it might be. High school

sports gave me a lot of resiliency and discipline. I learned how to grind it out. What's hard after you go through hell week in football? After that, things aren't that difficult in life when you've overcome such a hard thing. I developed this quality for not quitting, maybe a stubborn quality at times, but it was good for my well-being and mindset. I learned too that you only grow from conflict and struggle; you never grow when it's easy.

The time-tested idiom, "practice makes perfect," or its more refined and currently popular cousin, "perfect practice makes perfect," applies with full force in the field of athletics, and high school is no exception. It is well-accepted that top athletes in the world spend considerably more time practicing than they do competing. Repetition can produce mastery.

Athletes are exposed daily to drills designed to build muscle memory. Drills used wisely and correctly immeasurably enhance skills. Methods vary. Some coaches use the same well-planned drills most of the time, while others change up the drills to accomplish the same results. Some improvise during practices to adjust to what they see. But no matter what approach a coach employs, it comes down to repetition and trial and error, a process that high school athletes get to experience virtually every day of their season. The following is how a successful athlete and businessperson recounted that part of the high school sports experience:

> The first time you try a wrestling move, it's not going to work, and so you keep trying, trying, trying, trying, trying, and eventually it works. In rowing, the first stroke you take is going to be abysmal, but you practice and you practice until it becomes second nature. I did the same drills for the Olympic tryouts that I did in high school; I did the basics. What do guys do in basketball? They dribble, they shoot free throws, and so on. The drills in high school are probably the same as the drills in the NBA at the highest level. It is about getting the basics down and, when you get it wrong, figuring out what you can do to get better. It is dogged pursuit of your gold standard.

Each day in practice, coaches push athletes to make each moment count and develop sound habits. Coaches remind players that a missed moment in practice because of lack of attention or less-than-full effort is a missed opportunity to improve, moments that cannot be recaptured, and in the long-term, they can, if recurring enough, keep performance submerged beneath the excellence level. Coaches push their athletes to treat every moment as a separate challenge, to ignore what happened before, and always "be in the moment," like the lacrosse coach who told his goalie that the only shot on goal he needs to stop "is the next one." That dialed-in focus on what is happening in the now is, as the prior quoted athlete stressed, the "dogged pursuit" of excellence. The experience is a proving ground for the prospects of employment and performance in the workplace, as one former athlete, who has enjoyed a successful legal career, described:

> Organized sports aren't get-rich-quick activities. They require extensive preparation and practice that have a variety of culminating moments building on each other. In the workplace, people with that type of background tend to show up big time and have the discipline to follow through on what they say and give their best. They have high standards. They are invested in the outcome. If excellence is your benchmark, get surrounded with people from competitive athletic backgrounds.

We are not born experts. Expertise requires hard work during a long period of time. To achieve long-term success, an athlete must not only love their sport, but also be prepared to devote well-organized, seemingly endless hours working on their skills. A willingness to pursue that path, as well as endure the fluctuations of setback and recovery, can become a formula for a promising future beyond athletics. The pursuit of consistency in excellence is the ultimate teacher of self-responsibility and source of deep pride. Like perfection, it may not be achievable in the absolute sense. But it provides the drive to elevate performance to the highest practical levels to fulfill potential. The habits that produce excellence at the high school athletic level can endow athletes with a standard for performance embedded in whatever activities they undertake during a lifetime.

· 11 ·

The Power of Limits

Out of limitations comes creativity.

—Debbie Allen, actress, dancer,
choreographer, and television director[1]

We are in an important league game and the referees are tweet-
ing whistles more than usual, meaning they are calling a tight
physical game and letting little go. Because my team plays physical, the officiating pattern doesn't please them and frustration
sets in, leading to bad decisions and loosened team cohesion.
At halftime, I remind them of a basic game principle: "Control
what you can control. And, one thing you can't control is the
officiating, any more than you can control fans in the stands." I
urge them to focus especially on their emotional reactions and
adapt their style of play to what the adults with the whistles are
doing. I put three principles prominently on the whiteboard:
"controlled action," "discipline," and "adjustments." The second
half showcases a different team, as they respond well to the
halftime monologue and bring home the win. In the postgame
meeting, we explore more studiously what it means to stay
within the limits of what we can do, with specific references to
game moments where they executed the control principle well
when tested and played to their strengths, and how, as a result,
the team was able to determine its destiny.

$\mathcal{R}$ather than conquering comfort zones to break through to the other side
of talent, sometimes we are better served knowing what we control and acting
within our limitations. Well-defined control of what we can do leads to efficient and effective performance, and keeps us focused on our goals, whether

short-term or long-term. Conversely, falling to temptation to venture outside what we control can lead to frustration and often failure, perceived or real.

Sharon Melnick, author of *Success under Stress*, pointed out how stress often arises from what we cannot control and how we can limit our stress by accepting and honoring the outer limits of what we can control. Similarly, Vicki Phillips, a leading educator formerly with the Gates Foundation, in commenting on Daniel Goleman's groundbreaking ideas about emotional intelligence, wrote,

> He emphasizes the importance of self-efficacy—the belief that you are powerful because you can control your reaction to what happens to you in life. He believes that we can teach students to understand the link between their thoughts, feelings, and behavior, and help them see that they always have choices about how they will respond to any situation.[2]

Our limits are tested every day. A lawyer, for example, cannot control how a judge runs a courtroom, only the arguments the lawyer makes and the case the lawyer presents. None of us can control what others think of or feel about us, only what we let trigger us and how we behave in their presence or deal with them. We cannot control traffic, only how we respond to the complications it often tosses our way. We cannot control the weather, but we can control how we prepare for and respond to it. We cannot control the beliefs of others, only what we believe and offer them to consider in contrast. The list can go on.

When athletes are able to focus on their strengths and what they do best, they begin to develop an internal power of efficiency that maximizes output and success. It allows them to push to the side distractions that might otherwise put them off course. The meditative quality inherent in that focus is essential, even if the athlete doesn't fully appreciate the intricacies of the mental process at the time. What they learn at some point is that their ability to stay within the lines of their capacity leads to success, and when they stray, they tend to falter or at least compromise effective performance. Here is how one diligent high school lacrosse athlete, in tune with his internal processes, approached it:

> The skills that gave me my greatest edge as a player and are most prevalent in my life concern mindfulness as a player, including visualization and meditation. I learned that there are controllable aspects of the game, like your performance, and uncontrollable aspects, like the field condition or the weather or the hecklers. And the more you focus on the uncontrollable conditions, the more your stress level rises and the lower your performance. I try to see most everything in life that way now.

An important—and often underappreciated—benefit of high school athletics (and sports in general) is emotional control. High school coaches regularly urge their athletes to honor what they can control and not get caught up in what is outside their reach, as demonstrated in the opening scenario. The list of things players control and coaches exhort their athletes to stay focused on can include preparation, effort, work ethic, willingness to learn (coachability), active participation in team decisions, commitment, attitude, reactions to adversity, emotions, body language, eating habits and diet, staying fit, expressions of gratitude and positivity, and performance within the parameters of skill sets.

Conversely, coaches stress that athletes can't control officiating, fans, parents, and opponents. Nor can they control coaching styles or the rules that govern the athletic program. The most effective teams stay true to the limitations of what they can do. When guided properly, athletes learn, throughout time, the value of honoring these sorts of limitations. From a psychological perspective, it distills to self-awareness and self-honesty, knowing strengths and weaknesses, and being honest about them. It entails a clarity of mind that frees the athlete to concentrate on how they produce the results they seek and achieve the realistic goals they set. A former high school crew member and wrestler described his take on that process:

> High school sports allowed me to play to my strengths. I was the smallest kid, not athletic at ball sports, although I was okay at soccer. I tried to put a square peg in a round hole. I figured out what I was good at—combat and endurance-type painful sports—and I played to my strengths for the rest of my athletic career. In business, my experience in the navy, and even my marriage, the time I spend in meaningful situations outside of sports, I have benefited from knowing the importance of limits. The decisions I make as an adult playing to my strengths is something I learned in high school.

Reverting to the prior words of John Wooden, student-athletes need and, equally so, crave discipline. Student-athletes want rules and boundaries, even as they grumble about them. Structure bounded by team rules informs what is acceptable and expected, creating an atmosphere that is reassuring. Contrary to what some might presume, self-discipline, certainly in this context, isn't a negative force. It is a pillar of unwavering success that manifests in perseverance and the power to control impulses and avoid temptations that might erect barriers to attaining goals. Self-discipline is at the top of the list of attributes needed to achieve excellence in most anything we do. In athletics, at the high school level, self-discipline provides athletes a focus and pace that allows athletes to fulfill potential in the long-term. High school sports align mental and emotional energies, and, with diligent work, empower athletes to control actions. In the words of legendary Chinese philosopher and writer Lao Tzu, "Mastering others is strength. Mastering yourself is true power."[3]

There is a more subtle learning experience that attends adherence to limits in athletic performance: the development of trust. Frequently, athletes are asked to trust the judgment of their coaches. Student-athletes in high school have their fair share of strong-minded youth who, not so infrequently, believe they know a great deal about the sport they play. Sometimes they do, and many times they don't. In either case, however, the judgment of the coach overrides, and when it happens, coaches expect their athletes to trust their decisions. Adherence to things athletes control and the accompanying exercise of self-discipline often highlight that dynamic. Of course, it can backfire, for coaches sometimes make mistakes. But more often than not, their insistence on honoring limits rings true, and when athletes unconditionally follow that lead, they learn to trust the process and the judgment of people more experienced. That is not to say they can't question. Of course they can, and should whenever appropriate. It means that trust is another learning lesson for the athlete.

An athlete who honors their limits, focusing on strengths, demonstrates several characteristics that set them apart and help round their character. Honoring limits submerges pride and ego in favor of efficient performance, sacrificing today for the greater good of tomorrow and embracing the means over the ends. A Chinese proverb is relevant: "A journey of a thousand miles begins with a single step."[4]

> *A*n athlete who honors their limits, focusing on strengths, demonstrates several characteristics that set them apart and help round their character.

High school athletics have the benefit of regular exposure to the lesson that acting within the limits of control is empowering because it not only brings efficiency and maximizes success, but also helps align expectations with reality and minimizes or eliminates frustration and disappointment. An athlete who knows they have performed well within the parameters of their capabilities, maximizing effort and displaying a positive and encouraging attitude, will reap increased confidence and contentment, and know how to channel action efficiently and effectively, a nice base for adult life.

Effective Communication

Communication leads to community, that is, to understanding,
intimacy, and mutual valuing.

—Rollo May, psychologist and author[1]

A player of mine is having difficulty with his head coach in another sport and at a loss about what to do. He is frustrated. We
sit down one afternoon to vet the underlying issues. It is plain
after a few minutes that there are two at-odds perspectives. The
challenge is to find a way to bridge the gap to get coach and
player on the same page. I point out to him that the most effective approach out of the gate is to honor what the coach wants
to accomplish with the team and affirm that as a member of the
team, he is unconditionally committed to work for the better-
ment of the group. That way, I point out, the coach will see him
positively and as someone who wants to pull in the same direction as everyone else. It is important, I stress, to set a positive
tone for the conversation, despite existing frustration. I suggest
he use questions to get the coach's perspective—and thus give
the coach plenty of space to provide his viewpoint—and, of
course, for him to listen well to the answers. After hearing from
the coach, he can provide his perspective, including how he feels,
and he should strive to avoid being defensive, complaining, or
being accusatory. A week later, he tells me that he and coach
"are all good" and he is back on track with the team.

Effective communication is a life skill that never tires of improvement. It
defines the quality of personal, social, and business relationships, and fosters
understanding and empathy, shows respect, enhances discussions, improves

listening skills, and nurtures sustained growth in relationships. The ability to communicate effectively is a form of power, not in the political, business, or any pejorative sense, but in terms of the ability to impart information and perspectives in ways that entice the genuine interest of an audience. It is a skill that aids us in every walk of life, whether getting a job, performing on the job, or pursuing almost any life goal. No relationship can succeed or flourish without good communication. On the larger scale of a global economy, where competition for market share is rapidly increasing, the ability to communicate effectively is essential.

Communication in high school is multidimensional, covering personal interactions, team interplay and coordination, verbal and nonverbal expression, a customized sport language, and exposure to public commentary. Each is essential to the inner workings of a sports program, and each enjoys numerous learning opportunities.

To begin, high school athletics provide extensive opportunities to develop communication skills on an individual basis. High school athletic programs, for example, include one-on-one meetings between players and coaches during the season to review progress, address individual performance and expectations, and, sometimes, explore personal matters. Those moments are rich with opportunities to nurture communication skills. Far too often, however, adult–adolescent communication is a one-way process, even when the adult is well-intentioned.

For all the chatter of high school students outside the lines of athletic programs, whether on campus or elsewhere, adolescents generally are not great communicators, which raises the ante for coaches to teach their players how, why, and when to communicate. At base, players need to know that coaches value what they have to say. The breadth of communication benefits a high school sports program entails includes not only a conscientious focus on developing underlying communication skills, but also an atmosphere where discussion and personal engagement are valued and genuinely encouraged. Effective communication—what we want our youth to start to learn before they become adults—is a two-way street. It is collaborative, mutually respectful, and affirming.

An effective approach for many programs is an open-door policy where players know they are free to speak their minds without fear of reprisal or judgment in a relaxed and nonthreatening atmosphere. Vibrant programs encourage players to find different ways to initiate communication, whether by text, e-mail, or even through a teammate, to set up face-to-face discussions before or after practice or another time that works for both player and coach. Face-to-face discussions, although difficult for some players, are almost always the most productive way to gain clarity, be heard, and address concerns, especially if coaches genuinely commend players for coming forward to put their cards on the table.

Once that door swings open, direct conversations are easier. Every individual on the team, regardless of their role, has to be understood on a motivational level, and from there all communication must be based on their personality type. While many outside of sports may assume coaches don't get involved in the personal lives of their athletes, coaches understand they are ideally situated to assist athletes with personal and confidential issues, while respecting privacy. Taking a player to lunch, for example, is one of many effective ways coaches can communicate with their athletes in a relaxed atmosphere, allowing both coach and player to let their guard down enough to enjoy engaging and candid discussion. A program falls short whenever a player has something to share but can't find a way to share it. A program that encourages open communication avoids problems of that nature and generates cohesion among the team; minimizes misunderstandings among teammates, especially between coach and athlete; and helps build tolerance.

Coaches are called on to develop and religiously implement a communication value system. This includes emphasis on such principles as knowing your audience; not being defensive; looking people in the eye; and being a good listener, affirming, compassionate, and empathetic. Coaches can teach listening and talking skills by first modeling the role of the empathetic and open-minded communicator, and then providing student-athletes the chance to express themselves openly. Modeling these principles enables athletes to develop lasting communication skills.

Coaches are sometimes challenged to ensure that nonverbal communication lines up with their express words. Saying one thing that sounds like another can be problematic. When words and nonverbal cues don't line up, they create a dichotomy that forces athletes to choose between two arguably competing meanings. When they do align, coaches are clear and trustful. When they don't, the athlete most likely hears the nonverbal part of the communication more than its verbal counterpart since the former is more difficult to mask and representative of how coaches feel. The same is true with tone of voice. Coaches, it bears repeating, are always "on." Like it or not, how we communicate with nonverbal expressions models how we expect our athletes to communicate.

Team meetings on various subjects, including resolving team issues, discussing strategy and scouting information, eliciting personal observations about team experience, and, commonly, discussing game situations and performance, provide additional opportunities for players to express themselves, even though sometimes reluctantly, in a judgment-free environment.

Positive and effective communication within a high school sports program can create a family-quality bond. It is a connectiveness that impacts everyone involved in the experience and makes lasting internal marks. It holds the potential to create closely knit groups and special relationships, and makes it easier to get things done and solve problems.

The unique team bond also helps nurture social skills, notably learning to receive feedback without having self-confidence dismantled, clearing the way to share information to improve performance. It is not, admittedly, always easy and can be especially sensitive during the adolescent years, when thin skin prevails. But the advantage high school sports have is that feedback is a constant ingredient for how programs operate, and with the appropriate coaching values and temperament, it can be received as an integral and accepted part of the process. Coaches have a powerful platform to create a hungry learning environment, which includes direct feedback and constructive criticism as valuable tools. One multisport athlete described it this way:

> High school sports are not wanting for feedback and criticism, constructive and not so constructive. Athletes are exposed to tough commentary about performance, which prepares them for challenging communications down the road. Athletes learn how to "deal with it" in a way that allows them to move on and take feedback in stride, rather than sulk around and get down on themselves.

*P*ositive and effective communication within a high school sports program can create a family-quality bond.

On the athletic level, communication in high school sports is an essential ingredient of team success. An accepted high school coaching truism is that a talented team that communicates poorly will underperform and a less-skilled team that communicates well will overperform. That includes both verbal and nonverbal communication, and individual and team communication. To underscore its importance, coaches often allocate precious practice time to communication in drills. The following is an illustration of the team communication dynamic from a former high school football player:

> The most intriguing communication we had off the field was in film study sessions, which became more a conversation between coaches and athletes, and it could get intense. Film often doesn't lie, and it is not fun to get decimated in front of teammates when you screw up. But it

became more of a conversation along the way, and the back-and-forth improved listening and speaking skills, for which I am grateful. I learned much about how to communicate, about not being defensive and how to acknowledge mistakes and then figure out the most straight-line path to improvement. There were times when I disagreed, and I had to figure out how to walk that line where you don't sound like a defensive little shit but have a point to make at the same time, be respectful, and say, "You know, actually, here's what I saw on that play. Here's why I think my response was correct," and then let the chips fall where they may. I have lived by that approach ever since.

There is also a different form of communication in high school sports. According to the Association for Applied Sport Psychology, 70 percent of human communication is nonverbal, and arguably this figure is even higher in competitive sports.[2] Every sport in high school (and at other levels) has its own way of communicating what a player or team should do in game situations. A breadth of verbal and nonverbal communication is introduced at the high school level, which means a major item on the high school coaching agenda is getting athletes to communicate with one another in competition, especially where coordinated play occurs. While this will vary from sport to sport, coaches nonetheless stress that "team communication" is a separate skill that must be consistently practiced and honed for a team to compete well, and, toward that end, task players to communicate with one another for game advantage. Hand and various other signs, for example, are used to indicate what a player is supposed to do on the playing surface. The communication matrix of high school programs tends to include signals complicated and varied enough to minimize chances an opposing team can pick them up. The connection this creates is subtler, as it often turns on nonverbal cues and "reads" between teammates. It is a constant feature of high school athletic competition, as this former soccer player noted:

> A big advantage of team sports in high school is that it requires everyone to interact in a way that forwards the efforts of the team, meaning you have to learn collaborative communication. You have to communicate constantly with teammates and share responsibilities. You also have to speak up for yourself. In competition, you learn quickly that the team cannot function well unless everyone is in tune virtually all the time. It brings a level of comfort to ask for what you need or tell others later in life, because it becomes second nature in social and business settings.

The extension to the nonathletic adult world is manifest. When we interact, we give and receive wordless signals all the time. Our nonverbal behaviors—in the form of gestures we make, how we sit, how fast or loud we talk, how close we stand, the extent of eye contact—send messages. Even when not speaking, we give off signals nonverbally.

Another relatively unique communication dimension of high school sports is that teams often have their own language, some more complex than others. Each sport in high school athletics introduces a new lexicon for an athlete to master, and if the athlete participates in more than a single sport, more than one. The sports lexicon breeds connectiveness, improves camaraderie, and generates pride, which, in turn, translates into results in competition. The coded language of football, for instance, was highlighted in Kostya Kennedy's compelling book *Lasting Impact: One Team, One Season. What Happens When Our Sons Play Football*:

> Consider specifically football's elaborate lexicon, so sprawling and nuanced it might fairly be called a language of the game: words, phrases, code words, code phrases, intonations, and verbal cues that are all but unintelligible to those on the outside. Men and women on a small fishing vessel may talk of knotting their beckert hitches and cleaning the livewell; car mechanics may banter with one another about ball joints and the overhead cam; doctors and lawyers have full-blown dictionaries to contain and explain their terms of art. Yet, football provides unique linguistic adventures. The common language gets altered, evolving to fit each tribe, then each clan.[3]

The same can be said of several other sports, although the football dictionary is arguably the most complex. In all cases, however, the ability to communicate in what is for all intents and purposes a novel language prepares athletes for the many ways the workforce facilitates production through code and other coined phrases and words.

In addition, some (albeit not all) student athletes get the chance to talk to the media. It is a special experience that introduces athletes to public commentary. High school athletes get interviewed commonly these days, which fosters a different brand of communications skills, as they must be more selective in the words they choose and aware of the potential impact of how they express themselves, considering, in particular, that reporters are wont to parse words and create impressions the speaker didn't intend. The process can be unpredictable and sometimes must be handled delicately. Public comment for attribution is not a time to be flip. It falls on the school administration, especially coaches, to provide guidance on how student-athletes should (and sometimes when not to) speak to reporters and journalists. At a minimum, student-athletes who have media experience learn to be more comfortable in the public setting, which fosters ease of expression and provides perspective on the power of language. One former high school athlete, whose job often places him in the public arena, said when he talks to reporters now, he feels at home based on his experience in high school talking to the media. He added, "Being able to understand the context of those relationships which are very different than those of players and coaches, or teammate or opponent, and understanding that, I think gives you a maturity and a poise that you may not get in other things."

High school sports give athletes a boost along the never-ending quest to develop effective communication skills. Student-athletes are uniquely exposed to a spectrum of raw emotions and thus have opportunities to communicate within a diverse assembly of situations. They participate in activities every day that value and stress the importance of effective communication. As athletes, they use a separate language to communicate. They get to talk it up often and with vigor. The impact their communication experiences will have on how they function in adult life can be felt in the workplace, among family, and within the ambit of romantic and social relationships, particularly when in combination with the development of self-advocacy skills and the infusion of self-esteem. There is much development left for sure; we each are in that position. But high school sports effectively initiate the development of communication skills applicable to a wide range of adult relationships and public situations.

Decision-Making

It's not hard to make decisions when you know what your values are.

—Roy Disney[1]

After a devastating early season loss, as we leave the opponent's gym, an exasperated sophomore informs me she is quitting the team. Our opponent overwhelmed us with relentless pressure the entire game, and the frustration of the experience rattled her to the point of wanting to give it up. I first acknowledge her frustration, which I tell her is understandable in the circumstance, especially since I feel precisely the same way. I affirm that it is her decision to make and I will respect whatever she decides. But I recommend strongly she not take such a leap while reeling from the emotional turmoil of the moment, but instead let things calm down during the weekend and, once they do, gauge her feelings. I offer her guidance along the following lines: "Consider asking yourself some questions. For example, as practice approaches each day, do you feel rising enthusiasm? When you arrive at practice, are you thrilled to see your teammates? When practice is over, do you usually feel accomplished and good about yourself? When you are in the game, do you hate coming off the floor for a substitution? Do you feel connected to your teammates? Do you love the game? If the answers do not enthuse you, maybe this is not for you. If, on the other hand, they do, consider whether what you are feeling now is anxiety about failure, embarrassment, or the scary challenge of a steep hill of improvement." On Monday, she arrives for practice and says that on Saturday she overreacted to frustration, and the inclination to quit was a hasty reaction to a personal challenge. She goes on to become a team captain as a senior.

*O*ur choices establish our priorities and define us. We face decisions every day, from the mundane to the impactful. We sometimes make decisions with nary a thought and sometimes are afraid to make any decision, which is merely a different form of decision. The quality of our life reflects the decisions we make, placing a premium on informed and thoughtful decision-making.

Incisive decision-making is an art honed from experience. The more we engage in self-awareness-based decision-making, the stronger we become in figuring out what is best for us. It is an imperfect process, if for no other reason than sometimes matters outside our control intervene to lay waste to the best-laid plans. But within our control lies the ability to make increasingly sound decisions throughout time. At the end of the day, sound decision-making is about identifying what is important in our lives relative to competing interests—classic prioritization—projecting the likely results for the available decisional paths and crafting an action plan.

High school athletes repeatedly face decisional forks in the road during their sports careers. Coaches commonly press athletes to think thoughtfully about their athletic expectations and make conscious decisions about what they are willing to do to meet them. That way, they can establish priorities, set goals, and formulate realistic and rational expectations. It is a way to develop a value system. Here is an example from the lead player of a high school tennis team who found she had to choose between competing loyalties:

> I learned to make tough decisions in high school. The most difficult concerned a conflict between the SAT exam and a major state tennis match. Although I had scored well on the SAT the first time around, I needed to take it again if I wanted to improve chances of getting into colleges at the top of my wish list. I sat down with my parents and said, "What am I going to do? This is such a predicament!" After back-and-forth and soul-searching, I decided my college choices were more important than how my tennis team fared that weekend, and I decided to take the SATs again. The responses were split: "I can't believe you decided that" and "Good choice!" The decision foreshadowed other decisions I would come to make about which schools to attend, as well as how to deprioritize tennis in my life relative to certain other things. It has also helped me understand decision-making in business, especially with the startup work I have done, and how I see different stages of decision-making, like what I need to do to get to goals, and then be diligent and disciplined until I'm positioned to arrive there.

*H*igh school athletes repeatedly face decisional forks in the road during their sports careers.

Decision-making for high school athletes particularly comes into play with time management, a core skill for all student-athletes. Time management requires organizational skills, discipline to avoid distractions, efficient use of travel time to and from team events, using weekend time smartly, recognition of limitations, and insight into when the athlete performs certain tasks best. While all high school students face time management challenges, the student-athlete bears a special burden owing to the significant time and physical responsibilities a demanding sports program imposes. It can sometimes be a rocky road, no question, and student-athletes sometimes stumble, particularly in the earlier years of their high school sports careers, as they adjust to the more demanding academic and athletic requirements. In the long haul, however, student-athletes have ample opportunity to learn how to carry multiple major tasks and make decisions about how to handle the load. Coaches tend to be vigilant in reminding athletes of this special responsibility and can face situations where an athlete has failed to carry the burden well, which provides an important opportunity to reinforce the decision-making principle as it relates to time allocation and choices. The experience can be rewarding, as it was for this high school soccer athlete:

> Decision-making in high school athletics was highly beneficial. For instance, handling heavy academic loads, which I had, and the obligation to spend countless hours on a sport, time management became a major undertaking. I practiced three hours every day and had to figure out how I was going to get everything else done, especially schoolwork and family obligations. For me, it was a constant, "How do I want to tackle that?" As an adult, the same questions arise each day, and the process for me is the same. "How do I prioritize?"

A common decision high school athletes face today is whether to specialize in one sport or become a multisport athlete. It is no minor decision, as it has several implications, including college selection, long-term athletic goals, impact on academic performance, social life and time management, the breadth and variety of experience, the influence of parents, social relationships and friends, and the risks of burnout and injury. A good illustration of what a student-athlete faces when deciding where to give their athletic attention is this rendition from a talented soccer and basketball athlete who had a major decision to make:

> Probably the most difficult part of high school was deciding on which sport to concentrate. My passion was basketball, but my chance for a ticket to a college scholarship was soccer. I can't tell you how many discussions I had with my parents, older brother (who faced the same dilemma), and coaches about the pros and cons of the decision. I'll be honest. It was difficult. As a teenager, my vision was shorter term. But our discussions opened me to see the wisdom of thinking beyond high school, thinking long-term about my future. I decided to play both but played soccer year-round and often arrived at basketball practice either late or pretty beat because of the soccer commitment, much to the annoyance of my basketball coaches. In addition to the decision paying off in immediate dividends—I got a college ride for soccer—the lessons were invaluable, particularly the value of forward-looking in making decisions.

Sport selection has become especially acute for football, which while remaining popular has suffered a decline in participation because of documented concerns about the long-term health risks associated with head injuries, among other problems. More than ever, parents and their kids are discussing whether to play football at all, a discourse that combs the landscape of risk–reward like no other decision in high school, save perhaps college selection. The process is not unique to football, although the stakes are greater. In some ways, football has become the poster child for debates about sport selection in high school.

On a more general level, when student-athletes elect a sport, one decision they face at the threshold and continuously thereafter is the nature and extent of their commitment. For example, a common discussion between coach and athlete is how hard the athlete is willing to work and the kinds of things the athlete is willing to undertake to progress individually as an athlete and a contributor to team success. It is not uncommon for coaches to talk incessantly about what it means to be committed to the team and the sport, including the sacrifices and prioritization necessary to maximize contributions and fill potential. Sure, some players merely show up, with predictable results. The other end of the spectrum is an "all-in" commitment where an athlete is unconditionally dedicated to achieving the best results possible. The commitment continuum implicates core decision-making, as it did for this basketball player:

> The major decision for me was whether to commit to basketball in high school, not simply to play it, but to commit to the program. That meant devoting major portions of my summer, giving up winter break, working

most days in the offseason lifting, and focusing on my fundamentals. It was a huge commitment, and with the help of my parents, I was able to prioritize what was important to me in a way that made me feel good about my decision. Once I decided to commit to a degree I thought the program called for, the sport became my focus, and the risk–reward, advantage–disadvantage process I did with my folks provided me with a model for making important decisions as an adult.

The key is making conscious, well-considered, and informed decisions that leave as little to chance or error as possible. The other aspect—and much work here is required, especially for parents—is accepting the consequences of student-athlete decisions. Regret can be a powerful comeuppance. If an athlete doesn't commit in a way that is reasonably calculated to achieve stated goals, the consequences of disappointment from the course they chart are on them. It is not enough to be fully engaged in the decision-making process. In fact, the process is largely wasted if the decision-maker is not prepared to accept the consequences of what they decide. If a player wants a certain role on a team, for instance, but fails to spend the time to fill that role, the responsibility for a bad result lies primarily with the player. That is a vital lesson. An athlete who makes a major decision regarding their participation in athletics and accepts the consequences of the decision has taken a major maturity step toward understanding the value of conscientious and responsible decision-making.

One aspect of high school sports implicating decision-making, which coaches can do more to emphasize, is the fleeting nature of the high school sports experience. In the greater scheme of things, the experience doesn't last long, especially when considering the tiny percentage of high school athletes who get to play for college teams. Most statistical analyses show that about 2 percent of high school athletes go on to play for a college team, at all levels. This makes high school sports a diminishing asset. They are here one day and gone the next. It is a sobering reality that places a premium on student-athletes thinking long and hard about commitment to their high school sports programs. If thoughtful, they are faced with making decisions calculated to maximize participation benefits and minimize having later to regret shortsighted decision-making. It is a reality that wasn't lost on this high school basketball player:

> The interesting aspect of high school sports is how fleeting it is. You have to decide, consciously or not, whether you are going to capitalize on the moment. High school sports are here and gone quickly. It is a great opportunity, and missing it could cause great regret down the road. I learned that how I handle this diminishing asset reflected my priorities and decision-making preferences. It was a powerful lesson about consequences of decisions.

It is fair to observe that coaches don't work enough with athletes on self-awareness. It is a focus we each can stand to spend more time on. Lining up actions and decisions with an honest understanding of core personal values is an ongoing life challenge. Coaches are urged to do more in this area, as acute self-awareness is what generally leads to contentment. The athletic environment is well-positioned to encourage athletes to weigh their options thoughtfully and make well-considered decisions.

Competitive sports enhance decision-making skills in subtler ways. During game competition, athletes consistently face decisions moment to moment, like audible play-calling or player positioning in football, making play decisions in basketball, where precisely to send that penalty kick in soccer, finding that unreachable spot to place the ball during a volley in tennis, what golf club to use in a particular circumstance, and so on. These types of decisions are based on both information discernible in the moment and accumulated from experience. Athletes are often called on to process information in fluid situations and learn to make decisions quickly. Those types of decisions are not the conscious pro and con life choices athletes make in other contexts, but they are decisions nonetheless, tactical ones. Joe Ehrmann, in *InSideOut Coaching*, commented, "Sports develop the brain and, in particular, the reasoning capacity of the brains of young athletes as they learn and master plays, techniques, and formations, and learn to make split-second decisions."[2]

The ability to make split-second decisions with confidence can be quite helpful in the business world. Consider the perspective of this former high school lacrosse and football player, who became a successful investment portfolio manager:

> I constantly have to make decisions in the trading pit, much like a quarterback in the pocket. And like in football, they are split-second decisions about what to do, except there is often substantial money on the line. There has been a definite carryover between my football days in high school and trading in terms of handling pressure and making quick decisions.

The same skill can apply to routine events in everyday life. A former high school soccer player explained how the spontaneous decision-making she had to make in soccer has served her well in everyday life:

> One decision-making challenge in high school sports occurs in the heat of competition, constantly assessing everything that is happening around you in the moment and making instantaneous decisions. It is a skill learned from habit and enhanced with focus. It applies to many things we do, including driving, dealing with unforeseeable things that occur in

conversation or otherwise, and a host of other circumstances, in each case requiring that we process information quickly and respond. Organized sports, especially in high school, grounded me to handle those moments.

When high school athletes move on from high school, they will have enjoyed a wide range of opportunities to improve their decision-making skills. The challenge for coaches, parents, and other involved adults is to help the athlete make decisions in a conscious and self-honest way, and not based on instinct and habit, and to accept responsibility for outcomes.

Hope and Belief

The Elixir of Athletic Competition

Turn your face to the sun and let the shadows fall behind.

—Proverb

There are five minutes left in the game, and we are down 16 points. By most any measure, it's time to sit the starters and give others opportunities to play. Or is it? I call timeout and take a different tact, offering only these words, which I deliver in slow cadence to eager eyes: "We have the skills to come back. We are easily good enough. That, gentlemen, is not debatable. What we need is to be bold; we need to believe we can pull this off. If you believe, then we can do this. Let's go do this." Facing prospects against all odds, the antithesis of hope, the team hits the floor with a vengeance, astonishingly chipping away slowly and steadily at the enormous point deficit. The more they chip, the more hope they amass and the less confident the other team becomes. As they inch closer, the gym becomes increasingly frenetic. Still, the task seems more than ambitious, as they have expended so much energy, and, more problematic, there is only a minute left and they are down six. Miraculously, they close to within two and have the ball on the last possession. We get a good shot—and miss—and lose by two. In the postgame locker room, after the exhilaration ebbs some, I am clear on what happened. "We may have lost the game of points, the contest of the scoreboard, but we won something far more valuable than a basketball game. We won the challenge of what is possible and passed the test of accomplishment against all odds. You were special tonight. Let this achievement stay with you forever."

*H*ope is an abiding aspiration that breathes life into what is possible. Hope inspires us in different ways to confront problems head on with a sense of optimism, even if guarded. It gives us reason to keep going. We may not know how to handle the task at first, but when we have hope, we know enough not to give up.

Belief is what our internal monologue says we can accomplish. It fuels fortitude to stay the course regardless of perceived roadblocks. Potential is often not realized because of self-imposed beliefs about what can and can't be achieved, whether in career development, the workplace, academic settings, and sports, among other circumstances. The reality is that whatever someone thinks of themselves and how they perceive their abilities will typically determine outcome, a self-fulfilling prophecy.

In athletics, hope and belief are nuanced versions of a similar sense of an outcome. Hope encases the possibility and desire, and belief denotes confidence that a result will happen. In sports competition, we all hope for a positive outcome. Hope is prerequisite; without it the effort is futile. But having a sense of what's possible is not enough. Athletes must believe things can happen. It is an entirely different matter when teams and their athletes believe an outcome is likely to or will happen, that they can accomplish the goal despite long odds. They experience a different type of empowerment. In the words of leadership guru John Maxwell, "When you have hope in the future, you have power in the present."[1]

When they team up, hope and belief are formidable forces in high school athletics. If committed athletes operate in an environment of optimism, they will harbor the hope necessary to persevere, and if they believe they can achieve their goals, they will expend more effort and be more focused to increase the likelihood of success. Teams need talent to win, of course. But the difference maker is not always talent. Sometimes, it is the perception, the belief that success, however measured, can—and will—happen. A consuming belief in success infuses commitment, which lights the way to excellence in performance and builds a trust that the team has a good chance to make "it" happen. "One of the biggest predictors of success in athletics, and life in general, is confidence—the expectation that you will succeed," says Jonathan Fader, a sport psychologist and author of *Life as Sport*.[2]

The athletic seasonal journey is full of ups and downs, course inversions, thrills and disappointments, and successes and failures. Athletes are tested constantly in their ability to stay the course and keep motivated. As the parade of tests continues, athletes have golden opportunities to develop and sharpen mental toughness. The emotional rollercoaster can unnerve and become an impediment. But having healthy doses of hope and belief stored in their hearts and displayed in their attitudes can pace them steadily toward their goals. Therein lies the challenge, but the lessons are meaningful and enduring. Coaches who set realistic standards and expectations, encourage risk-taking, even embrace failure, and remain positive and upbeat despite setbacks help instill hope and belief in athletes and reduce or eliminate fear. High school athletes can develop a unique ability to persevere in the face of unfavorable odds. Call it a competitive sense, if you like. Call it mental toughness or the fear of losing. But no matter what label you use, high school athletes have a replenishing reservoir of hope and belief always available to them to summon.

At the high school level, coaches have the privilege of helping to instill strong belief in success through skillful facilitation of how an athlete handles situations. As one coach said to me, "An important part of the coaching mission is generating self-belief and connecting with realistic self-assessment and goals—all of those things have to come together to have a successful experience and program." Again, coaching technique is crucial. When coaches ask players to rise to the occasion, have they also prepared them for the cherished moment? There is no "how-to" here. It is a matter of knowing personnel and figuring out how best to empower them.

A former high school soccer player shared how his coach taught him and his teammates about empowerment and belief through a story his coach likes to tell about Duke University basketball coach Mike Krzyzewski. The setting was the 1992 NCAA East Regional final between Kentucky and Duke, held in the Meadowlands. With 2.1 seconds left in overtime, Duke, down one, had the ball under the Kentucky basket. The game seemed over. To win, Duke had to advance the ball to the other end of the floor in two seconds with a catch-and-shoot off a long pass and a game-winner at the buzzer. There was literally no margin for error. The key was a successful floor-length pass. Here is how he described the way his coach taught the lesson of empowerment and how he transferred the learning to his leadership role in management:

> Coach K didn't tell inbounding passer Grant Hill what to do. Instead, Coach K posed a question. He asked him, "Can you make the pass?" Empowered by the question, Hill said yes. Hill could have said no and forced a different approach, but Coach K gave him the room to believe in himself. He empowered his player. It was the difference between command and inspired influence. The rest is legendary. Hill threw an unobstructed pass three-quarters of the floor into the waiting arms of Christian Laettner, who caught the ball cleanly and, after a fake, made a turnaround jumper at the buzzer for the win. I adopted this facilitative management

style in my business world. When our social media company had a major developmental crossroads, rather than use an independent contractor for a fix, which many urged that we do, I asked my staff if they could solve the problem on their own. They said they could—and they did.

High school athletics sometimes generate hope of quite a different kind. Consider this story about a devoted multisport athlete who, early in his Pennsylvania high school career, was diagnosed with kidney complications. After the diagnosis, he felt his life was effectively over. After getting the necessary transplant, some doctors advised him to move on from sports to protect his fragile new addition. On the surface, that made sense. He was often fatigued and spent countless hours in the school nurse's office. Yet, he insisted on attending track and basketball practices, and, in fact, didn't miss a single practice in three years. Why? High school athletics were life for him. They gave him hope. They gave him the reasons he needed to live and get healthy. The thrill of competition, the joy of camaraderie among teammates, and the challenges of physical endurance gave him the promise of a healthy, normal childhood. Sports became his hope lifeline.

The power of hope and belief in high school competition is real and commonplace. Most sports teams and athletes experience situations where, to succeed, they must discard the logic that a desired result is statistically improbable in favor of the fervent belief it can happen. They must not only hope it can happen, but also believe it will happen. Here is an example for the ages.

In 2017, underdog Lick-Wilmerding High School (Lick) of San Francisco faced heavily favored St. Patrick–St. Vincent High School (SPSV) of Vallejo in a nonelimination California state playoff basketball game. SPSV had several college-bound athletes and was expected to win by 20, if not more. To make matters worse, game location was in the unfriendly confines of the SPSV gym, and worse still, Lick was down two starters to injury, including a defensive stopper. A betting person would have mailed it in. At the end of the first quarter, SPSV led, 20–5. It seemed men had taken the floor against boys, and the blowout was on. Although by halftime Lick managed to narrow the gap to 10, midway through the third quarter, the deficit ballooned to 20, the largest delta of the game. Again, the game seemed over. Somehow, however, Lick managed, again, to reduce to lead to 10 after three quarters. But try as they did, Lick couldn't lower the deficit to a manageable number, and the differential fluctuated between 10 and 15. As it was, the Lick team was playing spirited ball, some might say over their heads. Nonetheless, the Lick head coach, Eliot Smith, continued to rally his troops, marching up and down the bench, focusing his cheerleading energy not so much on his more talented players, whom he trusted to do what they capably could do, but more on the usual bench riders, who were being pressed into service more than normal because of the injuries. The coach wanted them to believe in the improbable. Coach Smith later described his thinking:

> My job is to create that hope for every boy and girl I coach, so that they understand they have the power, they've always had the power. In any sport, you're trying to build their confidence. And you're competing, so you can't give up, you can't quit, you can't justify. Win or lose, they have to believe in themselves, and that is the lesson of a champion.

Regardless, he had a tough task, for with 1:40 left, Lick was down nine and, again, seemed done. The survival of their life raft turned on the prospects of three consecutive three-point plays and three consecutive defensive stops at the other end in the final six possessions. What were the odds? They seemed longer than improbable; they seemed on the cusp of impossible. Tossing those odds to the winds, however, Lick managed to pull off both, hitting three consecutive perimeter shots and managing to protect the other end of the floor defensively, taking SPSV into overtime. In the extra frame, Lick, now in control, had its way, dominating the visibly stunned SPSV team and netting the W (over a team that would win the state title weeks later in its division). Score a victory for hope and belief.

Coach Smith had a vision. He may not have shared that vision with his players expressly. But he demonstrated it. He expressed his vision through infectious enthusiasm, encouragement, and confidence. He captained the ship of hope and belief, and, by his actions, invited his players to join him for the ride. It was inspiring to watch it unfold. No high school experience outside of sports can compare with what happens to youth who experience an uplifting experience of that magnitude. It fills young hearts with the passion and drive to overcome obstacles that might turn others away. Players and coaches alike rejoice in this aspect of high school sports. When the miracle that isn't a miracle happens, everything seems possible.

When sheer belief in the possibilities is internalized, its power knows few bounds. It becomes a mindset. For sure, a Lick–SPSV game experience, which enlarged the lesson, will not happen every week or even every year. But those moments do happen, whether directly to a team or other teams within viewing distance. On a more sustained basis, it is about culture and how coaches convey confidence and possibility in the challenges sports teams face. The lessons endure, as they did for this former athlete and current college athletic director: "My high school experience changed me in this respect: I learned that if you believe in something, you can figure out a way to make it happen. That has stayed with me throughout adulthood and is a mainstay of how I approach my work as college athletic director."

*H*ope and belief dispense with worries about being handcuffed with futility.

The beauty of these logic-defying experiences is that they are transmittable throughout time. Players who learn to overcome the improbable are quick to share their experience and perspective. Those stories have the quality of lore. While there are exceptions, of course, coaches love to pass down their wisdom and imbue others with passion and the belief that most anything can happen. It is one of the awe-inspiring aspects of athletics at all levels, including in high school. The following is one example from a high school coach:

> My high school coach stayed consistently true to his coaching principles, especially this one: No matter what the circumstances, each of us could get the job done. I have taken this with me in all that I do, especially the work I do with kids who have the deck stacked against them. When those kids overcome obstacles because they believe, I enjoy incredible satisfaction, an enduring sense of fulfillment. Maybe that's selfish. Maybe there's a selfish perspective there that you're almost doing it for the rush of seeing your kids succeed. I love to win, but winning comes in a lot of different forms. I remain focused with a passion on seeing kids succeed and helping them become contributing members of the community. That doesn't happen without my belief in them and their belief in themselves.

Hope and belief dispense with worries about being handcuffed with futility. That is a powerful place to be. High school athletes swing on the hope–belief pendulum on a regular basis. Unlike their peers, they get to dabble in an emotionally charged environment where overcoming the odds of success and climbing steep performance mountains are common fare. When the lessons of hope and belief are internalized, they produce a force that can rouse an invigorating life. That's quite the benefit.

· *15* ·

Conflict Resolution

The formulation of a problem is often more essential than its solution.

—Albert Einstein[1]

After I suspend a junior player temporarily for conduct detrimental to the team early in the season, she stuns us all by quitting. She is a skilled athlete and seems to love the game, and we didn't expect her to quit. The next year, as a senior, without advance communication, she shows up at tryouts as if it were business as usual. After quickly getting direction from my athletic director, I permit her to try out without fanfare. We are talented, and her addition will increase our chances to make a bona fide state title run. There are, however, unresolved issues from last year and continued bad blood between her and the team. As a result, I do not feel free to bring her back without their blessing. After tryouts formally conclude, I arrange for the team to meet without her to resolve the problem. I tell them the coaching staff will attend the meeting as observers only. I let them know there is no right or wrong answer and urge them to be open and honest about how they feel, focusing on what is important to each of them as players and a team, including chemistry, team values, the impact on team prospects, forgiveness, and whatever else comes to mind. The discussion is far-ranging, heartfelt, and eye-opening for me, as additional issues come to light I hadn't known. As I listen, I become worried more than ever about team chemistry if she returns, but deep down I harbor the hope the team finds its way to forgiveness and a second chance. After more than an hour, the team elects to take a vote—the coaches continue to remain silent—and unanimously decides against bringing the player back. Despite my (unexpressed) disappointment, I understand, respect, and honor their decision.

$\mathcal{C}$onflict resolution skills are an important asset in the portfolio of life skills. Many of us, however, lack the basic skills necessary to resolve conflicts that arise in life, from the routine to the momentous. The lack of dispute-resolution skills can be seen at every level in every pocket of our culture, from the political to the social to schools to families to romantic relationships. We seem more inclined to knock heads or bury them in the sand rather than facilitate compromise or resolve conflict wisely and with empathy and compassion.

The difference between having and not having conflict resolution skills, however, can be the difference in whether, for example, a personal relationship survives, a family relationship functions well, a lawsuit gets resolved with relative peace, a business moves forward effectively, someone keeps or loses their job, politicians find fair and balanced solutions to constituency problems, and discrete situations open us to experience empathy and renewed respect for others. Conflict resolution tests our ability to recognize and constructively respond to what matters to others, keep emotionally under control, be respectful in our reactions, have capacity to forgive, and move genuinely past underlying tension. It opens us to deprioritize some conflicts as not worth the time and energy, and commit to resolve others by exploring common ground and compromise. In a nutshell, having and exercising such skills makes us happier, more independent, and functional.

In its most general sense, in a group setting, conflict resolution is a natural consequence of managing others, whether on the job or as a coach running an athletic program. In the action-packed, emotionally high-pitched atmosphere of high school athletic competition, conflict is bound to occur. Indeed, conflicts are commonplace in the competitive environment. The emotional and physical intensity, combined with the pervasive desire to win, is natural fodder for eruption between personalities. While we should strive to minimize the times it happens, the fact is, it happens and will continue to happen. The key is using the opportunity to teach conflict resolution skills. The inevitability of conflict puts coaches in the driver's seat to understand, recognize, and manage conflict in a positive and productive manner. Conflict resolution is a learned skill like others student-athletes acquire during their high school sports career.

Each coach has their style about how to approach conflict. As a general matter, the process typically entails allowing everyone involved to provide their perspective without interruption, followed perhaps by questions to clarify, seeking to find common ground and generating problem-solving options, and, finally, finding consensus or agreement. As part of this process, when applicable, coaches, in modeling behavior, should never underestimate the power of an apology to restore trust and formulate reconciliation.

*C*onflict resolution is a learned skill like others student-athletes acquire during their high school sports career.

The upside to teaching student-athletes how to deal with conflict is considerable. The give-and-take process of sharing differing perspectives and learning to listen and be heard are major maturity steps. Other benefits include tolerance, better trust, interpersonal harmony, closer relationships and cohesion, increased motivation, clarification of intentions and behavior, and a better team environment overall. In addition, sometimes athletes learn that conflict can be resolved peacefully without altercation of physical confrontation and that it is counterproductive to engage a conflict with the intention to change other's opinions or win an argument. The process of resolving conflicts also affirms the core values of the athletic program, whatever they are and however prioritized.

Probably the most common conflict that arises in high school sports springs from skewed perception. For example, a player might believe their coach is punishing or making a negative value judgment about them because of the minutes the coach allocates to their playing time or substitution decisions the coach makes during competition. Those types of conflicts are the easiest to tackle and resolve, as basic communication and clarity are the trick.

Another is the garden-variety interpersonal conflict that arises between two athletes or sometimes between coach and athlete. It is not uncommon for two high school students to have tension between them, especially in the competitive sports realm. Oftentimes what seems like a personality clash has to do with something brewing beneath the surface, like competition for a role on the team. These conflicts can be difficult to resolve, but, again, communication and clarity of feelings are key.

Less common—but in the mix—are conflicts that arise concerning tangible items, for instance, a dispute about use of equipment. These should be relatively easy to address, and if they can't get resolved amicably, the coach can impose solutions. More problematic is a situation where one athlete is accused of stealing from another. Those are rare, take on an entirely different panoply of considerations, and tend to be "above the pay grade" of the coaching staff. Still, the lessons and impacts involved in that eventuality can be far-reaching.

Conflicts also arise from values, rules, and principles. The most common is where parents complain about the manner in which the school or coach specifically imposes discipline or metes out consequences based on a violation of school policy or rule. For example, assume a player, in a moment of frustration, disrespects a coach with abusive language. There the resolution might focus on creating understanding about what is important in the program and what triggered the conduct, and not necessarily compromising rule application. Fairness, too, is always a consideration.

Research shows that although many adolescents lack necessary social skills to interact constructively, problem-solving skills can be taught to students.[2] Generally, high schools give scant attention to developing skill sets that facilitate conflict resolution, except in remediation of specific one-off incidents that occur. High school athletics, however, continuously present situations in which players, coaches, and teams must resolve disputes and conflicts that arise during the season. They are invaluable and can take many forms.

Parents may, as noted, raise concerns about how coaches are handling certain players, necessitating a meeting with the parents, player, and coaches. Coaches might ask captains to recommend how to handle rule violations in discrete situations. Games can present conflicts between players and officials, and coaches and officials. A coach might have to intervene in and facilitate resolution of a specific alteration or ongoing tension between two or more players. A team might be forced to decide how a player who has violated team rules should be disciplined. Similarly, coaches might need to resolve with the team whether to punish the entire team because of the transgression of a player. The team might want to confront the coaching staff about various program issues, for example, how practice is conducted or the effectiveness of an offensive or defensive system. The social interaction inherent in the athletic environment covers a wide educational berth for teaching athletes how to solve interpersonal conflicts and communicate with others in an effective manner.

Nick Holt of the University of Alberta and his research crew from the Faculty of Physical Education and Recreation studied conflict resolution by monitoring two competitive girls' soccer teams for one season. Holt and his researchers found that the girls learned to manage conflict at an adult level.

> The girls realized when someone was having an argument with someone else, and that it wasn't helping the team. So, they'd group together and try to mediate the conflict. In sport, you've got to work with the people you

might not get along with. . . . It's not about being afraid of conflict and just keeping everyone happy all the time; it's about encouraging the girls to deal with conflicts when they arise because those are growth experiences. Those things will transfer outside of sport, because that's what you've got to do when you start working.[3]

Again, individual player conflict is common. It can arise within the scope of personality disharmony, racial animus, and competition within the team. Player conflict also is common when team leaders believe someone on the team is dogging it, not contributing within capacity, or simply has a negative attitude harmful to the team. Sometimes the natural expression of keen and well-intentioned competition can be disguised as conflict. Coaches may let those moments pass since they tend to build camaraderie and may even provide fleeting entertainment. It is when the tension escalates into patterns that threaten the fabric of team cohesion or individual players have a serious personal issue between them where coaches or team leadership have to intervene to find tenable solutions.

A player who learns to handle conflict at the high school level in a mature and effective manner can enjoy long dividends, as was the case with this captain of her high school tennis team:

> We had many conflicts to resolve on my high school tennis team, a sport that sometimes draws prima donnas. As a leader of the team, I had to figure out ways to keep us on track without upsetting any apple carts. It was an experience that prepared me for the business world. One example from my business experience where my high school tennis experiences came in handy concerned a guy who had a propensity to hurl profanities at me and even threaten me, outrageous stuff, typically because of miscommunication. I didn't push back directly but parried and listened. I let the energy die of its own volition and didn't engage his ego, which freed him to come back the next day and apologize. That experience reminded me of the tennis team. Like my teammates, he was a contributor to the team. Like with my tennis team, I had to work this out somehow, even if it was awkward. I had to take a high road that gave him venting space, as I did my teammates, and then allow the power of his own energy to reverse his course of action, without confronting him directly and engaging his ego.

Sometimes the conflict is between player and coach. This can be challenging wholly apart from the underlying issues because of the inherent power imbalance. Players aren't always going to feel comfortable approaching a coach they believe is not acting fairly with them. It can be an intimidating situation. The difference in authority and power is not trifling, and coaches must constantly take that imbalance into account in dealing with their athletes. Being self-aware of such emotional and personal obstacles frees coaches to encourage communication when a conflict with a player is simmering. A quiet athlete doesn't mean a conflict-free athlete. Having an environment that encourages communication, as discussed in chapter 12, can break down walls between coaches and athletes, and spur dialogue crucial to solving problems. An athletic program that values self-advocacy and open communication encourages athletes to resolve conflicts, no matter how daunting. Parents, too, can help the athlete navigate the process and identify a resolution path that fits the student-athlete personality and addresses their concerns fairly. Consider this potentially explosive situation a high school football player had to handle:

> My freshman basketball coach was also one of the defensive coaches on the football staff. He was not a nice man, a bona fide rage-aholic, and racist and sexist, too. I had to figure out how to deal with the constant conflict his personality and value system set in my path, a tall task for a young high school athlete trying to stay focused on playing good football and doing well in the classroom. It taught me early that we are not always going to run across princes among men, and it was good to get experience dealing with the dark side. I had extensive discussions with my parents about the lessons to learn and how to navigate the relationship without running afoul of rules [or] protocol, or compromising my athletic and academic pursuits. I wound up just keeping my head down, as it were, not get worked up or take anything personally, and let it all roll off my back. I stayed focused on everything else important in the high school experience. The advice I received and the approach I used have stayed with me ever since.

It is common for all of us, coaches included, to dismiss some conflicts as insufficiently grave or worthy to warrant attention and intervention. While it makes sense for coaches to pick their spots in various contexts during a season, letting conflict go unaddressed can stoke turbulence, creating major individual and team problems. It is another situation where coaching priorities and time allocation come into play. What kind of program do you want? What are the values? As stressed throughout this book, coaches are in a powerful position to influence and have impact. No matter what the nature of the conflict, whether sprung from playing time complaints, personality clashes, physical intensity, and so on, failure to address the underlying problem can not only damage team chemistry, but also be a missed opportunity to teach important skills. What are the priorities?

The enduring lessons of conflict resolution in high school sports can be many. Athletes learn that conflicts fester and worsen, and cannot be ignored; conflicts on the surface often mask the real problem or actual feelings; conflict resolution yields emotional growth and builds mutual respect and acceptance; conflict resolution gives those involved a voice; forgiveness is a powerful personal act; we won't like everyone we meet but can learn to work well with most people; and compromise, balance, and common ground are meaningful. Not every long-term benefit will be available, of course, but some will, and athletic programs are well-served to confront conflicts head-on and prioritize the development of conflict resolution skills for their athletes. The road after schooling is littered with conflicts of all sorts, and there is no better place early in life to learn how to handle them than a high school sports program.

· *16* ·

Character

The essential thing is not knowledge, but character.

—Joseph LeConte, physician, conservationist, and geologist[1]

The season before, one of our players suffered a debilitating knee injury that kept him sidelined virtually his entire junior year, elevating the already-important senior year to a cherished level. He works hard to get ready for his high school finale and gets off to a great start. But a few weeks into the season, he reinjures the knee, a calamity that turns out to be season-ending, and thus high school–career ending. He weathers this abrupt and unceremonious halt to his high school basketball career in dignified silence but unconditionally cheers his teammates from the sidelines each game. After the last game of the year, with everyone gathered in the locker room, we ask each player to say a few personal meaningful words about the season. A fellow graduating senior, when his time to speak arrives, rises with notes in hand and begins talking, not about himself, but about his fallen teammate. He speaks tearfully about the courage it took, in the face of such disappointment, to endure the experience of watching teammates work hard each day in practice and sitting on the bench each game without any hope of playing the game he loves with his cherished teammates. He speaks eloquently, from the heart, tears still evident, about how everyone on the team has been fortunate to have him as a teammate and privileged to experience the depth of his character as he braved this monster setback without complaint or bitterness and with grace. He closes by saying the teammate is his hero.

*T*he face of character is moral strength and integrity. When character is well developed, it manifests through a commitment to act in accordance with personally held values. It draws people to us and inspires them to believe in and rely on us. Some say character is the most valuable thing we have, something no one can take away.

Character and success often go together. Researchers from the Center on Children and Families at the Brookings Institution concluded in a 2014 study, that on-cognitive skills and character competencies affect success as much as academic skill. Another study, drawing on research from neuroscience, economics, and psychology, found that such character traits as grit, curiosity, conscientiousness, and optimism are more vital to success than IQ, and can be taught by, among others, coaches and other mentors.[2]

The late John Gardner, former high school swimmer, member of the U.S. Marine Corps, founder of Common Cause, and secretary of health, education, and welfare for President Lyndon Johnson during the Great Society period, drew this connection between sports and character: "There isn't any other youth institution that equals sports as a setting in which to develop character. There just isn't. Sports are the perfect setting because character is tested all the time. It means a great deal if that time is well used."[3]

James Thompson, founder of the Positive Coaching Alliance (PCA), replicated this point of view in his book *Developing Better Athletes, Better People*: "Sports is a virtual classroom for building character with an endless procession of teachable moments—opportunities to teach self-confidence, resiliency, teamwork, empathy, mental toughness, self-control, and respect for others."[4]

*C*oaches who build programs that value the development of character play a pivotal role in the pipeline of future success for their athletes.

Student-athletes in quality sports programs experience moments virtually every day that touch on character. They are wide ranging and include *responsibility* as a teammate; *accountability* as a student-athlete; *dedication* to shared values of the athletic program; consistent *trustworthiness* in team interactions and performance; *fair play* when dealing with teammates and opponents; *self-control* and *civility* at all times; model *citizenship* when in public (see chapter 8); a strong *work ethic*; *pride* in the accomplishments of teammates, the team, the coaching staff, and the school; *humility* in winning and losing and competing; *unselfishness* as a teammate; *empathy* and *compassion* in situations involving the misfortune of others, small and large; *mental toughness* in difficult circumstances; *patience* and a sense of the right moment to act; and *leaving ego* at the playing facility door.

Coaches who build programs that value the development of character play a pivotal role in the pipeline of future success for their athletes. A character-based athletic program stands out and draws the attention of the community, including higher institutions. A reputation for delivering student-athletes into the world possessing sound character becomes a model from which we all benefit. As a bellwether of success at the high school level, it becomes a calling card, as this high school coach explained:

> When we talk about a successful program, we talk about where the kids are achieving academically better than their peers, who are socially mature, who are making good decisions both on and off the court, who are admired by their peers, and who are family people. We also talk about the responsibility our kids have to the community to be great role models. We talk about putting team before self, and we talk about a "we" culture, and that it's not just what's happening on the basketball court, but are you carrying it all into other parts of your life? Are you allowing other people to be a part of your world? Are you able to create situations where you are respecting, trusting, and impacting others to be the same? When college coaches are calling and asking about our guys, apart from academic achievement, do they want to know what kind of person is he?

Character doesn't always follow naturally from high school sports. Fundamentally, its development depends on adults, especially coaches, teaching values that lay at its foundation. This is where having a value-based system is most vital. It is also where coach self-examination burns for the greatest attention. A coach cannot facilitate the development of character—a moralistic-based human quality—without understanding his or her own motivations and behavior, and embracing themselves as a model for their student-athletes. As noted, throughout a high school sports season, never mind a four-year career, opportunities for coaches to teach character present themselves repeatedly. Unlike situations that present teaching moments for the sport itself, which often require prioritization because of time considerations, teaching moments that implicate character warrant keen coaching attention virtually without exception.

An important component of character is empathy, a quality tailor-made for development amid the ebb and flow of the high school sports experience.

In his inspirational book *InSideOut Coaching: How Sports Can Transform Lives*, former NFL player and inspirational speaker Joe Ehrmann wrote,

> [Empathy] is the broadest and boldest virtue that a coach can exercise. Empathy is the foundation upon which morality is built. The virtue of empathy, the understanding that what hurts others hurts us, is also part of the foundation for competition. . . . Empathy creates the foundation for a player to feel, know, understand, and be accepted for his or her authentic self. For young people to develop and learn empathy they must experience someone empathizing with them. Empathy is the building block of successful relationships. If boys and girls are to live an other-centered, cause-oriented life, empathy must be the guide. It is the antidote to injustice, apathy, and indifference to the pain and plight of others.[5]

Situations where coaches can teach about empathy are commonplace in the high school athletic experience. It can occur in the form of sportsmanship shown to another team on the losing end of a lopsided (or blowout) game. It can be implicated when a player shows up an opponent, either visibly or with trash talk. It can arise when a teammate suffers a bad competitive outing or commits a costly error in a game and is despondent as a result. It can happen as described in the opening scenario of this chapter when a senior loses the chance to play virtually the entire or a substantial portion of the season due to an injury. It might happen when a teammate suffers a family loss, for example, a grandparent or parent, and the coach marshals the team to give comfort to the grieving player. It can be presented traditionally in the form of service to others, for instance, a team outing during the season to a soup kitchen or homeless shelter, or as part of a fundraiser for disaster relief to help a community suffering the severe impact of a hurricane or destructive wildfire. It can be showcased anytime a coach sees the chance to help student-athletes visualize and project life in the less-fortunate shoes of others.

It is incumbent on coaches to identify moments when these opportunities present themselves and make positive and effective use of them to teach. One of the powers of competitive sports is how repeatedly they test athletes. It is hard to get through a four-year high school sports program without having some personally defining moments. Sports can be deeply impactful. They command the best from everyone involved and test limits at the mental, emotional, and physical levels.

James Thompson of PCA demystified the art of teaching about character:

> There is really no mystique to teaching positive character traits. It can be approached as you would approach teaching any skill. There are four basic

steps: (1) introduce and define the character trait; (2) look for opportunities to illustrate the concept as the season progresses; (3) reinforce, model, and intervene when appropriate; and (4) look for stories to share with the players.[6]

Coaches can model character for their athletes. At the threshold, coaches are encouraged to share their feelings and emotions with their athletes. How coaches deal with human-interest moments and adversity, treat their players, communicate with referees, deal with parents, practice the values they preach, and generally conduct themselves will, to varying degrees, influence the student-athletes under their charge. The impact might not be immediate or all-encompassing, but like the lessons of parenting, the infusion of influence often eventually finds expression in how the student-athlete conducts themselves as an adult. One brash young athlete, who became a highly successful professional, expressed the influence this way:

> I'm outgoing and effusive, but my high school coach was the humblest guy you'd ever meet, and he taught me the value of humility. He'd say, "When you win, say nothing, when you lose, say even less." Did I always follow those things? No! But he did imbue me with me a sense of humbleness I never had and now carry with me as an adult.

Most high school athletes leave high school infused with the core values and principles of their athletic programs. They are fortified with a sense of what it takes to succeed, armed with the confidence to meet the challenges ahead, and stronger emotionally than when they arrived as freshmen. The road is not always smooth. It sometimes requires earnest self-assessment and honesty, no minor undertaking for a teenager. But with the proper adult guidance, high school athletes can make major strides in personal growth, notwithstanding the pangs that come with it. Coaches don't do their players any favors by letting pass moments that may be difficult to handle because of challenging personalities. It is convenient to look away, of course, but a value-based system commends coaches to stay loyal to principles, in good and bad times. The short-term pain of confrontation and candor can be life-changing, as a tennis coach found in dealing with a strong-willed and obdurate athlete:

> Our star player, in the spring of his junior year, announced he wasn't going to play tennis that year because of some physical challenges and because, "The guys don't like me—they hate me." I responded that he didn't like them either, and this presented a major growth opportunity for him and them. He decided to play and wound up apologizing to his teammates for his imperious behavior. He had figured out the problem was his attitude,

always looking for perfection from himself and everyone else, and yeah, that's good, but to a point. It was remarkable personal growth for him to figure it all out.

No citation is needed to state that competitive sports both reveal and build character. It doesn't always work out positively. We can see what happens at the club level, with screaming coaches and parents out of control, instilling fear and resentment in the youth under their influence and creating harmful examples by throwing tantrums or pulling teams off the floor to protest officiating. Fortunately, high school coaches are in an advantageous position to teach positive values and articulate important life principles—to build character. The situations for application of these qualities recur. It is a matter of preparing the student-athlete to see the wisdom and worth of the wide assortment of accessible intangibles—integrity, fairness, honesty, respect, politeness, courage, loyalty, humility, empathy, compassion, self-discipline, and kindness. A high school sports program that emphasizes these attributes will deliver student-athletes to the world as burgeoning productive citizens who will spread positive influence wherever they go.

• 17 •

Learning the Importance of Mentors and Role Models

Being a role model is the most powerful form of educating.

—John Wooden[1]

I have taken a player under my proverbial wing, not so much for his athletic development, but to help ease the hardship of his home life, which makes it difficult for him to get by every day. He often comes to practice on an empty stomach and must fight many distractions outside of school merely to play catch-up, never mind keep pace with most everyone else. The struggle is steep, and change, realistically, can be expected only in tiny doses. He and I talk often about "life" and his dreams, which are ambitious given his situation. I never, however, discourage him. Rather, I seek to guide him to take small steps along potentially fruitful paths. Our relationship is up and down, since it is hard for him to be consistent, and I am challenged by the pattern of steps backward after hard-earned, small steps forward. While we have our trying moments, we hang tough together. One day he is uncharacteristically effusive, and as he gushes about a future life, he takes me aback when he says out of the blue, "Coach, when I become a father, I am going to help my children like you help me."

$\mathscr{R}$ole models for our youth are increasingly important in our complex and often confusing world. Good role models disarm, guide without judgment, bolster the spirit, are emphatic and compassionate, and, above all, inspire sound decision-making and deliver wisdom about life lessons and direction. The more role models help with personal development, important life decisions, and the search for contentment, the more thriving our communities

121

and successful our citizens. A substantial number of studies show that we learn through modeling others. Role models help uncover our potential and overcome barriers. They allow us to see more clearly our personal traits and beyond our faults toward problem solution and goal achievement.[2]

High school is a self-centered phase of life. It is a time when students endure varying degrees of alienation and need support and positive reinforcement, which can occur in various forms, including through mentorship. Otherwise, they can drift too inward. As they navigate the twists, turns, and speed bumps of the high school experience, teenagers often become psychologically distanced from parents, escalating the importance that others step up as a role models and mentors. Fortunately, positive adult role models can be found outside the family during this time of life, including teachers, sports coaches, and community leaders.

High school coaches wear many hats. One is as role model and another is as mentor. The role model function is inherent in the work of coaches and integral to the educational process of student-athletes. A coach can't make a move without throwing off some message, real or imagined. Everything a coach does, whether in the form of words, body language, or behavior, express or implied, communicates something. The unassailable reality is that coaches are always on the radar and subject to scrutiny, sometimes to a fault. In consequence, modeling behavior may be the most important aspect of what a coach does. It is where coaches are assessed for who they are and where coaching impact may be the greatest. Not surprisingly, the late John Wooden had an apt observation in this regard: "A leader's most powerful ally is his or her own example."[3]

The role model function is inherent in the work of coaches and integral to the educational process of student-athletes.

Student-athletes expect coaches to have their acts together. Coaches are held to a high standard, which creates presumptions about behavior and values. If coach behavior matches professed values, the system works as designed. Consistency between deeds and words breeds trust. Measuring overt behavior for consistency is easy. Does a coach treat players with the kind of respect players are expected to show others? How does a coach handle adverse moments in games? Is the coach professional and passionate or, in contrast, agitated and over-the-top demonstrative? How does the coach treat referees or officials? Is the coach respectful or does the coach blast game officials with incessant snide and biting commentary? What is the coach's tone of voice in stressful moments? Does the voice get raised nervously or with manifest irritation whenever a trigger moment occurs or is the coach more measured, albeit passionate? What behavior is the coach modeling?

Whether a coach is consistent with words and actions, however, isn't always self-evident to the casual eye. For example, if a coach harps on the importance of certain skills in game situations but doesn't allocate sufficient practice time to develop those skills, the game-time harangue tends to ring hollow. If a coach sets express standards for behavior in dealing with game officials or opposing fans and acts differently, whether in practices or games, the message is confused and undermined. Coaches can hardly expect their players to show good sportsmanship if they deride players in practice or, more publicly, officials in games. If a coach exhorts the importance of a strong work ethic but isn't working as hard or outworking their athletes, the coach is sending mixed signals. The same is true for enforcement of rules. Consistency is essential to clear messaging about expected behavior. Worse than confusion about messaging, these inconsistencies—and there can be others, of course—deflate the trust student-athletes want to have in adult leaders and can undo the fabric of program culture.

When deeds and words are aligned, however, which is the unbending goal, the results are enduring, as it was for this high school soccer athlete, who rose to become a Division I coach at a northeast university:

> As a young high school student, I wasn't secure within myself. I looked at my coaches and saw independence and confidence, and thought, "Wow! That's a person who I want to be like. That person has got their act together." My main coach was an inspiration. She cared and taught us values. She'd push us past perceived limits. She encouraged and, yes, sometimes intimidated, but she always had our best interests in mind. She wanted us to learn the limits we didn't even know existed. She taught me how to be a mentor and role model to others. I'm an educator. And I take great value and great pride in that. I am very careful how I handle things. Even the little things. I make sure I'm in shape. I'm not going to go out and tell them that they must be in shape when I'm not in great shape. I value how I present myself. I respect my players.

High school athletes also often serve as role models for one another. In a value-based high school sports curriculum, they do that by being courteous and polite to their teammates, coaches, game officials, fans, and everyone with whom they come in contact, especially in the community at large. In a well-handled program, they understand it is a privilege to play high school sports, which comes with an obligation to represent the team, school, and community well. Athletes emerge as role models in many other ways. They set good examples for teammates and others when they perform well academically, demonstrate tireless work ethic, are disciplined, show emotional intelligence, treat everyone with respect, and honor the rules of the program. Coaches should be quick to affirm these players, privately and publicly. By doing so, coaches advance the values and standards of the program for everyone and make a broad statement about the importance of role model behavior.

The mentoring function of coaches has a similar impact to that of role model, although its effectiveness assumes discrete skills and often needs training. One study found that when coaches mentor athletes, among other things, they develop "strong ties" that help student-athletes "achieve personal goals," in addition to athletic ones, and "nurture the development of" student athletes "in all facets of their lives."[4] Furthermore, a Big Brothers Big Sisters study found that kids who participated in mentorship programs were 52 percent less likely than their peers to skip school, 46 percent less likely to start using drugs, and 27 percent less likely to begin drinking alcohol. Moreover, a mentor helps develop interpersonal skills, increases self-confidence, and teaches such valuable skills as goal-setting and decision-making, which, in turn, improve academic and postschooling career performance.[5]

Schools can do more to provide mentoring training for their coaches. Some coaches are naturals. But many aren't as facile with the process of mentoring kids. Coaching and mentoring are not the same by any stretch. Coaching is more task-oriented and performance driven, and requires technical skills to achieve certain results. Grounded in trust, mentoring is relationship-oriented and personal development driven. It is where a coach offers guidance, support, and encouragement to help athletes develop character, make sound decisions, and acquire various life values. When mentored well, student-athletes have the chance to share their experiences by being a mentor down the line, as this volleyball player did once she became a college Division I coach at an eastern university:

> As coaches, we are teachers and educators. We are there to help student-athletes become the best volleyball player, student, and person they can be. And it's a little higher demand in the college realm, but it's the same philosophy: We're here to support them, we're here to help them grow, we're here to help them build into an identity. I think that one of the biggest things that I took away from my high school experience was just that support. It was always there.

A former multisport high school athlete, now an elementary teacher and high school coach, made a similar point:

I think high school athletic programs have a great opportunity to surround young people with mentors and responsible adults who transcend the title of coach and harness the value of teacher. The environment is ripe for great work to be done, and I think it's important that kids are surrounded by people who view their job through those lifelong lenses, good role models and mentors who can be impactful.

The beauty is when student-athletes absorb the value of role modeling and mentoring to an extent it becomes part of their identity and value system. Coaches who become effective mentors and role models for young athletes are extensions of family, the importance of which is plain. One former high school athlete incorporated the lessons of mentoring and role modeling from his high school coaches into how he approaches his management work:

> I spent so much time with coaches they became a second family to me, as were my teammates. Coaches guide you, and while they never did the work for me, they supplied me with the proper tools to get me where I was going. The same is true today in my job. I don't anticipate our vice president and CEO to do the work for me, but they do give me the tools I need to succeed, which is similar to coaching. I look to them in the same way I looked to my coaches, although when you're a kid, there's more hand-holding and drama and tears than in the real world, but I definitely feel like the things we did in high school shaped me to be the person that I am today. I know how to use the resources available to me and when to forge ahead independently.

Coaches have various resources available to encourage mentorship in high school athletic programs. They are not in this alone. Athletic programs often have buddy systems that pair more experienced athletes with those with less experience. A more responsible or experienced athlete might be asked to take a teammate under their wing to help with existing problems or challenges, for instance, time management and academic performance. Another might be asked to shadow a player whose family strife makes it difficult for them to carry their weight as a teammate.

Peer-to-peer mentoring among student-athletes contains extensive benefits. Among others, they include (1) increased self-esteem, (2) increased empathy, (3) improved social skills, (4) greater connection to the team and common mission, (5) enhanced conflict resolution skills, and (6) increased academic performance. There are potential downsides as well, one of which is placing too much responsibility on the shoulders of an adolescent, which places a premium on careful peer matching. On the whole, however, so long as the peer mentor focuses on model and positive behavior, and finding ways to help teammates improve, peer mentorship is a mutually beneficial way to teach the importance of mentoring and provide life benefits to matched-up duos. Peer mentors are also instructed on the boundaries of their new roles and on which specific aspects of the experience they should focus, with emphasis on role fulfillment rather than a specified or glorified outcome. In addition, a student-athlete capable of mentoring a younger, less experienced teammate can develop leadership skills and have impact beyond the mentoring relationship. Coaches are able to monitor these situations to ensure their effectiveness and take advantage of the skill development as it happens.

It is noteworthy in this context that a core principle of a well-considered high school athletic program is empathy-based support for those less fortunate or capable. When more experienced players act as mentors for other players, they not only show leadership skills, but also reaffirm the culture of the team and, in the process, make the team stronger. By carving out mentor roles among the team, coaches create opportunities for thriving relationships between and among players, and minimize negativity and status differentials. In the long-term, moreover, they instill in their athletes the core value of mentoring, which extends well beyond formal education.

The resources of local communities apply here. The community is rich with opportunities for student-athletes to acquire mentoring skills as part of the athletic program. Younger kids look up to high school athletes, which gives the latter prized opportunities to influence them at an early age and provide the student-athlete a valued experience as a mentor. For example, high school sports programs sometimes have their athletes visit lower educational classrooms to demonstrate athletic skills and share thoughts on the importance of academic performance, time management, sound work habits, proper social behavior, and specific life values. Another opportunity some schools use is having high school athletes act as officials in lower school athletic contests. There are many other ways for high school athletes to have mentoring involvement with students at the lower level. Commitment, creativity, and practicality are the guideposts.

One aspect of mentoring of high school athletes that gets scant attention is the aid given to student-athletes who vie to play collegiate sports. There are many organizations that specialize in assisting high school athletes to improve the chances of college scholarships or a favorable look as a walk-on athlete. Most are profit centers. But others provide that service through a nonprofit model, focusing on not only helping athletes improve their pedigrees as competitive athletes, but also developing the kind of character colleges value in good citizens. Take, for instance, Student Athletes in Touch (S.A.T.), which operates out of Texas and California, under the leadership of coach Michael Bobino, a former instructor of Sports Psychology at UCLA and dean of academics at JFK High School in Richmond, California. Bobino founded

S.A.T. in the 1990s, with an essential mission to "provide a mentoring program that bridges the gap between high school and college . . . and also build character, responsibility, and teamwork with the student-athlete and the parent." One testimonial, from an Atlantic Falcons executive, lauded the program as a vehicle that helps student-athletes "better themselves."[6] Mentoring programs like these have a long-term impact on character development and the value of mentoring.

Mentoring and role modeling in high school sports are a valuable part of the educational experience. For the high school athlete, mentor and role model relationships present opportunities to experience life lessons outside the bounds of the traditional classroom that can't be derived from textbooks and lectures. Mentoring is an effective way to transfer skills, and role modeling plays the same role for values and behavior. Both place a premium on how adults handle the constancy of moments where those lessons are ripe, and both bear substantial upside in the growth of student-athletes, especially in laying a strong, value-based foundation for their futures.

Health and Wellness

To keep the body in good health is a duty, otherwise we shall not be able to keep our mind strong and clear.

—Buddha[1]

Jeremy displays a repertoire of basic basketball skills, one of which is a long shooting range. He is limited, however, because of a lack of intensity and physicality, which impacts the energy he throws off and makes him inconsistent and often ineffective in games. He has a slight build and shies away from contact. I give him the "your body is a temple" talk and suggest a weight building and nutritional regime to make him stronger and more resilient. I tell him that regardless of what happens with the basketball program, developing a routine that pays allegiance to his body will likely become an important lifetime habit, and he will be well served to lay a strong conditioning foundation now. He takes the advice to heart, gets strong, and over time his play in competitive situations improves considerably. More importantly, long past high school, he continues his workout regimens, which have become more refined and in tune with modern training developments. He has a well-entrenched long-term commitment to taking care of his body.

$\mathcal{T}$he importance of physical fitness and sound nutritional habits are beyond question. They help decrease risk of disease; make us feel better physically and mentally; and help us look better, avoid injury, and, not the least, live longer. The *American Journal of Preventative Medicine* reported that regular exercise can increase longevity for as many as five years. A study discussed in

Proceedings of the National Academy of Sciences in December 2009, found that being physically fit at age 18 increases the likelihood of higher-than-average educational and professional achievements in adulthood. Other studies attribute such positive outcomes to physical activity as a sense of purpose, a better quality of life, improved sleep, and reduced stress, as well as stronger relationships and social connectedness.[2]

Conversely the lack of physical activity can mean increased anxiety and depression; higher risk of such preventable illnesses and conditions as high blood pressure, coronary heart diseases, diabetes, osteoporosis, colon cancer, and obesity; and lower life expectancy. Some studies indicate a sedentary life is deadlier than smoking and that physical nonactivity contributes to some noncommunicable diseases (e.g., heart disease, diabetes, and certain kinds of cancer). According to a paper by Harold Kohl and Heather Cook, entitled "Educating the Student Body: Taking Physical Activity and Physical Education to School," the lack of regular exercise at an early age can increase the risk of cardiovascular disease.[3]

High school athletic programs instill a regimen of physical training and respect for the body. The major conclusion drawn from a study entitled "Sports Participation and Health-Related Behaviors among U.S. Youth," published in the *Archives of Pediatrics and Adolescent Medicine* in September 2000, is that sports programs promote positive health behaviors and deter negative health behaviors because they value health and fitness as integral to quality sports performance.[4] Indeed, studies consistently show that high school athletes develop healthy habits for their bodies that carry into adulthood. They show that teens who participate in sports maintain higher levels of physical activity in later years; are less inclined to become smokers; are more inclined to develop good eating and lifestyle habits; and are less at risk of diabetes, heart disease, obesity, and other chronic ailments, as well as stress, depression, and suicide ideation. And, unlike in the classroom, high school athletes develop fine and gross motor skills.[5]

High school athletes learn early the importance of physical fitness and, equally important, that good training habits are essential to maintaining physical fitness. Competitive sports in high school are not PE classes once or twice a week. Fitness is integral to the world of the student-athlete during the school year and for most of the offseason as well. Staying in shape, for them, becomes a way of life. Habits that cultivate fitness become rooted, laying a foundation that can last a lifetime and pay untold dividends throughout the remainder of their lives.

The following three comments from former high school athletes—football, basketball, and soccer, respectively—could apply to most high school athletes:

My high school football experience taught me what it takes to be in condition and stay that way. Seeing the cause and effect with respect to effort followed by physical outcome was a powerful lesson and something you don't forget. I've drawn on that countless times in my adult life and attribute much of my attitude toward physical health to the relentless work we did in my high school football program.

Now that I'm 10 years removed from high school, while it's not easy to stay in shape, I am constantly reminded I did it in high school. And although I probably will never be able to devote the same hours I put in then because of job responsibilities and other real-life things that get in the way, having been raised as an athlete, I have learned the value of staying in shape and maintaining a healthy lifestyle. High school sports gave me a benchmark, so to speak, for physical fitness and conditioning.

High school sports taught me the value of being in top physical condition, which has come in handy when things in life don't go well and you hit bumps in the road. The ability to maintain a strong body—which is traceable to extremely tough workouts in high school—has been my saving grace in coping with loss of family and the challenges of being a mother of two. Along with my music, working out and staying fit is religion to me. It never fails to get me through difficult times. In high school, we had to confront our weaknesses head on. We had no choice. We had to bring our best. I have always found pushing myself physically to the brink liberating. Now, no matter what is on my plate, I am going to bring it. Sports and fitness are insurance policies against a crappy life.

Taking care of the body is not only a recipe for good physical health, but also much more. It feeds protein to the mind and gives us a connected wholeness to our entire being. Mind–body connectedness is not a modern concept. The ancient Greeks took the view that the human body should never be neglected in the pursuit of higher education. They believed that our minds and bodies are inseparable and that physical fitness should be an end of itself for the benefits it bestows on the mind. Plato, for example, emphasized the importance of bodily exercise for developing the mind. He sought to establish a harmonious conflation of body, mind, and psyche. Apropos, the ancient Athenians adopted as their own the Roman motto, which is attributed to the Roman poet Juvenal, "Mens sana in corpore sano" (A sane mind in a sound body).

That perspective prevailed until the 17th century, when the Western world began to see the mind and body as distinct entities. More recently, however, beginning in the 20th century, prevalent thinking reversed. Researchers began to reaffirm the mind–body connection and scientifically demonstrated complex links between the body and mind. Integrative psychiatrist James Lake of Stanford University has written, "Extensive research has confirmed the medical and mental benefits of meditation, mindfulness training, yoga, and other mind–body practices."[6] In the words of one licensed clinical social worker, writing for *Psychology Today*,

> Mind and body appear to be simply differing aspects of the same whole. As the head and tail of a coin are not separate, but differential points of the same coin, mind and body are thoroughly entwined and inseparable. Where one leaves off and the other starts is a consideration rooted in the outdated belief of cause and effect.[7]

The bottom line is that exercise and mental health are inextricably linked. Consider the words of Thich Nhat Hanh in *How to Love*:

> Body and mind are not two separate entities. What happens in the body will have an effect on the mind and vice versa. Mind relies on the body to manifest and the body on mind in order to be alive, in order to be possible. When you love someone, you have to respect her, not only her mind, but also her body. You respect your own body, and you respect her body. The body is you. Your body is your mind. The other person's mind and body are also connected.[8]

It is not surprising, then, that studies consistently show a direct causal link between exercise and significant mental health and emotional benefits. Exercise not only relaxes us, but also helps build self-esteem and self-image, and spurs us to be more productive. It invigorates our daily mood, creating feelings of happiness and even euphoria through the release of endorphins and the redirection of mental focus. Motor competence can lead to feelings of mastery and confidence in overcoming problems and challenges. Exercise increases concentrations of norepinephrine, which can moderate the brain's reaction to stressful situations and diminish or relieve anxiety.[9] Studies similarly show that exercise can lessen symptoms for the clinically depressed. Indeed, one study compared the effects of exercise with antidepression medication, noting that exercise now is one of the most recommended coping devices among healthcare experts. And while it is no cure for degenerative diseases like Alzheimer's, exercise has shown to help shore up the brain against cognitive decline and, in the process, create new brain cells and improve overall brain performance, notably enhanced memory.[10]

Recent trends in high school auger even better for the benefits of the mind–body dynamic in high school sports programs. The general trend in education to use meditation and yoga to address nonsocial behavior that interferes with the learning process—allowing schools to minimize or, in many cases, eliminate discipline—has expanded into high school sports programs. While the marriage of yoga and competitive athleticism is not new—Kareem Abdul-Jabbar, for instance, used yoga to enhance his considerable basketball prowess as early as his high school days, decades before the practice became a household name[11]—it has in recent years become of growing interest in high school sports as an institutionally accepted activity.

Initial skepticism about the utility of yoga as a mainstay of high school athletics, and its attendant typecasts about being hocus-pocus, limited to certain cultures, or a gender-specific activity, has steadily given way to the acknowledgment that yoga is hard work and, for many, the hardest physical activity ever undertaken. Beyond the physical challenge, yoga trains the body to move fluidly as an integrated unit, helps build concentration, prevents injury, and allows more efficient and powerful breathing, a bevy of assets that hold untold benefits for an athlete. On the personal side, it boosts self-awareness and self-esteem, introducing young and new practitioners to the power of self-introspection, which has a domino effect of breaking down barriers to improve relationships, especially with teammates.

One high school coach, who became a convert of the value of yoga for his players, described his perspective in the following way:

> When you coach, you always want to get a little extra edge on your competitors. Instead of wasting our time doing the same old things in offseason conditioning, I decided to focus on the core. Every fundamental movement in baseball comes from the core of your body. If you don't have balance, you're not going to have good mechanics, and if you don't have core strength, you're not going to have balance. What is the best way to get a stronger core? The research I've seen points to yoga.[12]

In addition, as one study has showed, yoga can reap positive psychological effects for high school students. According to a study in the *Journal of Developmental and Behavioral Pediatrics*, the official journal of the Society for Developmental and Behavioral Pediatrics, yoga may serve a preventative role in staving off mental health disorders, which commonly develop in the teenage years. As the study revealed, teens practicing yoga scored better on several of the psychological tests than fellow students who took only regular PE classes. In consequence, various school-based stress management and wellness programs have been developed with the goal of encouraging healthy coping strategies and resilience among teens with the aid of yoga classes.[13]

*H*igh school athletics lay the groundwork for a lifetime of honoring the body and serving the mind.

The companion to yoga practice is meditation, which also is finding its way into high school sports programs. Meditation is the source of body–mind mastery. Studies have shown that meditation improves motor performance, reduces anxiety, and increases calm and self-confidence, an asset for any athlete about to engage in a competitive contest.[14] Coach John Wooden often talked about how he never tried to stoke his players before a game and favored a calmer, more focused pregame atmosphere. Athletes generally perform better and with greater satisfaction when their minds are clear and focused. Beyond the benefits in the competitive realm, meditation is a valuable lifelong asset for well-being.

High school athletics lay the groundwork for a lifetime of honoring the body and serving the mind. For high school athletes, physical fitness can become more than a lifetime habit; it can define self-perception and become an identity. They can be proud to say, no matter their age, "I am an athlete." It is a great way to think and a reassuring way to live.

· 19 ·

The Positivity Culture

Perpetual optimism is a force multiplier.

—Colin Powell, former secretary of state and four-star general[1]

Apart from cutting players at tryouts, probably the most difficult aspect of coaching in high school for me was injecting genuine positivity into gloomy moments after demoralizing losses. I usually found the right words to say but sometimes struggled below the surface to line up my feelings with the content of the spirit-lifting postgame monologue. That challenge awaited me following a tough loss on the road against a league opponent, one of those games we were expected and needed to win for favorable playoff seeding. The postgame locker room, as anticipated, was cloud-ridden, with heads down and shoulders slumped. I wasn't far into my attempt to extract silver linings from the setback when the opposing coach—who I knew well and who, as athletic director, had given me my first high school coaching gig—entered the room armed with boxes of pizza. That magnanimous gesture, I don't need to tell you, changed the atmosphere immediately, and the best was yet to come. He knew what the mood was going to be like for us, and he knew what we needed to hear. As the team ravished the food—a welcome diversion from the dejection in the air—and he had the boys' rapt attention, he held forth, regaling us with how talented the team was, how destined they were for success, how fortunate the players were to have such dedicated and talented coaches, and how hard and courageous the boys had played that night. He spoke in glowing terms, as he was uncommonly gracious, kind, and

135

empathetic in victory and infectious in enthusiasm. Today, more than a decade later, people in that room still talk about it. It was one of the most powerful displays of positivity (and class) I had ever experienced and reflected the athletic culture he had built for decades where celebration of the human spirit in an upbeat and positive environment were its defining qualities. Leaving the gym that night, I never felt as good about so tough a loss. It was a night to remember.

The importance of positivity is not breaking news. There are innumerable books written on the topic and related subjects. There also seems an inexhaustible supply of inspirational quotes to fuel our motivation. In our culture today, there is such keen focus on the principle of positivity that some might dismiss it as a mere tagline or perfunctory rally cry. But positivity isn't a mere word. It is a force to uplift us in most everything we do and a profound vehicle to change how we live. Optimism is infectious. Upbeat people revitalize us, while downbeat people blow storm clouds our way.

Positivity isn't all about contentment. It's also about the energy that builds life skills and creates enduring value in our lives. Studies have consistently identified important life benefits flowing from a positive mindset. Here is a sampling: (1) more flexible thinking and resilient conduct; (2) deeper, more expansive and more connected relationships, including with family; (3) longevity; (4) increased creativity; (5) joy and cultivation of peace; (6) greater emotional intelligence; (7) healthier self-image and self-esteem; (8) increased hope and trust; (9) better physical health (e.g., lower blood pressure, decreased incidence of heart disease, better weight control, and healthier blood sugar levels); and (10) less stress and anxiety.[2]

It is accepted that brain activity influences the body, and when there is a health downturn, cultivating positive emotions strengthens the immune system and combats depression. A study published in the *Journal of Gerontology*, done under the auspices of the Yale School of Public Health, found that having a positive view about aging can enhance belief in abilities, decrease perceived stress, and foster healthful behaviors, as well as reduce levels of C-reactive protein, a marker of stress-related inflammation associated with heart disease and other illnesses.[3] A study at the Harvard T. H. Chan School of Public Health reached similar conclusions.[4]

In the context of high school sports, positivity implicates culture. When positivity is the basis for a sports program, it can imbue every feature of the athletic experience. Building a "sports culture" is a model for success. Today, the term *sports culture* is entrenched in our sports lexicon. It is a go-to reference whenever we try to explain the long-term success of a sports team or dynasty. Invariably, it is said, a history of winning means that program leadership successfully built a sports culture that celebrates a host of intangible qualities, for instance, accountability, commonality of purpose, discipline, trust, loyalty, selflessness, honesty, realistic expectations, and effective communication.

An athletic program expresses what its sports culture embodies regarding values and attitudes. The content of this book speaks in various ways to a thriving sports culture, for example, developing empathy-based character, affirming athletes to build self-esteem and confidence, overcoming comfort zone limitations, encouraging and nurturing self-advocacy, and believing in the ability to overcome difficult odds of success, among other qualities and benefits. When a sports program lives and breathes positivity, each quality and benefit of a valued-based high school sports program thrives, operating in tandem, creating expectations that what happens in the athletic experience will generate good feelings, bring varying degrees of fulfillment, and hearten student-athletes for the future.

> *A*n athletic program expresses what its sports culture embodies regarding values and attitudes.

It begins with language and what is said between and among coaches and players. A University of Michigan study, shared via the *Harvard Business Review*, concluded that a 5:1 positive to negative feedback improves overall effectiveness of strategic business leadership teams measured by customer satisfaction and financial performance. The main difference between high-performing and low-performing teams was the ratio of positive comments (e.g., "Great idea," "I agree") versus the negative counterpart (e.g., "That's not worthy of consideration," "I disagree," or sarcasm).[5]

It bears noting that *some* negative feedback is an important, essential part of the mix. Constructive feedback protects against complacency and commands attention. It also underscores the importance of positivity. As James Thompson of the Positive Coaching Alliance noted, "The paradoxical beauty of relentlessly positive coaching is that it makes criticism easier for you to give and easier for the player to accept. When feeling appreciated and valued by you, a player will be more open to hearing your criticisms."[6]

The ratio of positive to negative commentary has direct application to high school sports and is an optimal baseline for building a positivity-based sports culture. The ratio builds cohesion, cloaks the team with good energy, and enhances leadership skills. It can also alter the way they live their lives, as this high school hoopster learned:

> I spent time during two consecutive summers in high school at Point Guard College [PGC]. It was exhilarating for several reasons, but I got hooked on one of their suggestions, that we strive each practice to give six positive feedback comments to our teammates for every constructive comment—they didn't like "negative"—and that we keep a tally of how well we did, until the 6-to-1 practice became routine. What I didn't realize as much or at all at the time was that PGC was teaching us not only about how to be effective leaders on our teams, but also, via that formula, to become better and happier people.

It takes little coaching insight to conclude that a team plagued with recurring negativity foments an environment that diminishes the quality of competitive performance and a team culture built on positive energy enhances performance. Constructive criticism is more conducive to success than destructive criticism. It is not uncommon for kids to be hard on themselves as the result of habits of self-criticism they develop early in life. Coaches in high school have an important role in trying to undo those habits in favor of constructive comments that don't judge behavior, but celebrate the potential of change and improvement. We need to find better ways to give feedback and avoid being too hard on student-athletes. The era of tough love is waning, if not over.

A sports culture built on the strength of positivity broadens possibilities and, in turn, increases the potential to build new skills and develop new resources to succeed. Studies have shown that happiness has an upward spiral effect. Happy people more easily develop new skills that produce new success, which, correspondingly, brings more happiness, and so goes the pattern.[7] As coaches build cultures based on positivity, they create behavioral expectations. If clear and consistent these expectations inform athletes on how to behave; communicate; function as a team member; deal with one another, the community, and the public in general; and grapple effectively with conflict and other challenges they confront.

Positivity is, fundamentally, a mindset. When it thrives as the signature of a high school sports program, it is expressed in every nook and cranny of the athletic experience. It is, as discussed, most directly represented in the preponderance of positive comments coaches make to players and players make to one another, not the least of which is the tone of voice coaches use to teach at practice and urge in game competition, and teammates use to encourage, direct, and guide one another. It is seen in hugs, high fives, arms-wrapped-around shoulders, pats on the back, and whatever new bumps and choreography successive generations of student-athletes select to express their bonds and camaraderie. It is captured in how much teammates enjoy playing with one another and the game they have gathered to play, and in demonstrations of team morale, cohesion, and harmony. It is bounded in locker rooms filled with eager energy and game-ready temperament as the team gets dialed-in for the next contest. It plays out on the bench and sidelines in the different ways teammates support one another on the playing surface. It fills hearts whenever teammates are quick to support and show empathy to a teammate who has fallen, gotten frustrated, or become despondent. It shows up in how teams treat their opponents and honor fair play, and the respect they show officials. It fuels team optimism and gives extended life to hope and belief whenever teams face steep odds. It percolates in an endless stream of unexpressed contentment that passes through the minds and hearts of student-athletes during the athletic experience. And, above all, it makes everyone connected with the journey feel good about themselves and their common purpose.

Think about the sports programs you know. Is the atmosphere stress free or do they intensely border-on-edge? Are voices raised or soft? Do positive comments dominate over negative counterparts? Is competition in practice spirited or cutthroat? Put differently, do athletes work to make one another better or seek to one-up teammates? Are emotions expressed openly without judgment or do athletes repress how they feel? Do the coaches practice what they preach? Do most players seem to be having fun?

Atmosphere speaks volumes about the culture and its values, how cohesive the team is, and how committed teammates are to one another. A well-conceived sports culture entices everyone to support and propagate it. Positivity in sports values the importance of relationships and encourages resilience in structuring the athletic experience by giving respect to the views of others. Positivity expects everyone, coaches foremost, to listen well to what everyone involved has to say. In the end, a collaborative approach helps build the culture and gives each athlete a stake in its development and legacy.

Athletic directors and coaches are bound to lead the way in developing a high school sports culture defined by expressions of positivity. It doesn't happen otherwise. Adult leadership, especially coaches, must first model the behavior they want their athletes to mirror and, through that behavior, identify the values, attitudes, and principles they want as the foundation of the team culture. Aside from modeling behavior, coaches can talk up the culture so that student-athletes understand and place in real-life situations the core meaning of the value of positivity and begin to appreciate the heritage of which they each are a part. Without real context, we risk leaving the impression that posted sayings on the wall or whiteboard are no more than throwaway platitudes to motivate for a win.

Keeping an optimistic attitude and upbeat tone is not always easy. The competitive nature of sports can present a formidable obstacle to staying positive. It requires self-awareness and some honest soul-searching. Coaches, in particular, need be reminded of its importance, as it is easy to slip into frustration when engulfed in the throes of competition and pushing hard to improve. The following two high school athletes (basketball and football, respectively) gave useful reminders for coaches to hear:

> I didn't mind tough love in high school. It worked for me. But I had to have the love part and know that the toughness was about love. That can be hard to figure out as a teenager because we have so many antennae up and are so defensive. Looking back, I think coaches sometimes lost sight of how fragile and sensitive we tended to be, and how much impact they had. The truth is, I never tired of compliment, and I never tired of being around when things were happy and upbeat. I got it, totally got it, that we needed to be focused and serious, and had a job to do, but we needed to be playful sometimes too and not take ourselves too seriously.

> There has to be a line drawn where you can be a military marine-type person like my high school football coach and put kids through hell. If you keep the intention that it's all for their own well-being, maybe it can be okay, but it is when you start abusing the kids emotionally or mentally abusing them, that's when it crosses the line. And I experienced part of that. I think what I learned, certainly for me, but I think too for my teammates as well, you can be positive without fear of coddling and pampering. You can inspire through optimism.

On the flip side, it is heartening when coaches monitor themselves carefully and exercise ongoing self-awareness. It is even better when they acknowledge their slips and falls, and rise to the occasion of creating an uplifting atmosphere, as this coach of three decades is committed to accomplishing:

> I will be the first to admit, well hopefully not the first, that I sometimes allowed game frustration to blind me to teaching moments and the sacred trust I held to model good behavior for my players. Competitive sports, I think most would agree, bring out both the best and worst in all of us. Winning can be a powerful driving force, and coaches are challenged to keep focused on the larger issues that define our role. I know I can be. The good news is that I continue to work at it, and I encourage my coaching colleagues to do the same.

No question, coaching can be a smoldering kettle eagerly awaiting eruption into bursts of frustration. Is there any coach, at least beginning at the high school level, who isn't wired to compete with intensity, no matter how they express it? The emotional coaching meter can have a steep rise in the curve when game time approaches and even get enflamed depending on specific game circumstances. Staying poised, positive and under control—and thus clearheaded—is no easy task. Yet, no matter what happens in the competitive venue, no matter how frustrating and disappointing the competitive results, a coach can support his players. It is always an option. James Thompson stated, "The coach's number-one priority is to support her players, and it is the key positive character trait of a great coach."[8] Indeed, what greater demonstration of mental toughness is there than when a coach supports an athlete in the face of adversity or severe disappointment?

It is also true that coaches have limited time and aren't always trained in the ways and means of producing the wide swath of benefits available in the high school athletic experience. But coaches are center stage and will have considerable impact on their athletes, one way or another, like it or not. They are integral. It is not such a bad idea for high school coaches to probe internally to gauge the extent to which the emotional intensity they experience as coaches, whether in practice or more prominently in game competition, is, more than anything else, about their ego, a compulsion to project a personal identity defined by competitive results, or a desire to want more than what their athletes can fairly deliver. That degree of introspection, which doesn't always come easy, can be enormously meaningful and open a wide pathway to personal growth, especially if accompanied by the courage to own imperfections and flaws, and understand when those limitations can impede or tax the mentoring and teaching roles.

Coaches should be prepared for their players to recoil from too much positivity. It must, of course, be real, meaning the natural expression of core passion and commitment to principles. It can't be sappy and forced. Student-athletes respect genuineness, even if they don't embrace all the hoopla. The bet is that it will rub off and become part of their character throughout time, as happened with this four-year varsity basketball player:

> At the time, I thought all the rah-rah, positive talk in our high school program was a bit much. It wasn't that we didn't get to experience the down moments for what they were, but coach kept trying to get us to feel good about everything, to find something good in everything that happened. It was sometimes maddening to be around an adult who was so up and positive. But it had an impact that I didn't really see then but now appreciate. Coach was making us stronger, tougher, by being positive all the time. He was teaching us to be flexible and optimistic, despite setbacks and disappointment. It is clearer now. And it is how I try to raise my children. Thank you, coach!

Building a sports culture based on positivity makes the many other benefits of the high school sports experience pronounced, fluid, and effective. It opens everyone up to the possibilities and establishes an atmosphere that will often carry forward. One of the fallacies of high school coaching is that winning—and certainly consistent winning—requires that we compromise devotion to the other benefits of the high school sports experience in deference to maximizing the time coaches believe they need to teach their sport. It is, I submit, the opposite. When a value-based sports program is established under the umbrella of a culture cloaked in positivity, the prospects for winning are immeasurably enhanced relative to talent and skills. More importantly, the values student-athletes take with them upon graduation, after the joy of spending years in a pervasively positive sports environment, are victories for all time.

Conclusion (and a New Beginning)

I confess to some idealism. I painted with a broad brush in outlining what I believe are the essential features of a value-based high school sports system. I know that to do everything discussed in this book in all its splendor asks a lot from a lot of people, both in terms of allocation of time and changed habits and priorities. I am aware of how difficult it is to function as an athletic director, more so now than ever before. I know how much coaches care about the kids, how hard they work in running and building their specific sports programs, especially considering the avalanche of administrative responsibilities that fall annually on their shoulders, and how easy it is to get caught up in competition and lose perspective or balance. I am not insensitive to the stress of raising children in modern times, the pressures that bear heavily on parental responsibility, and the consuming and sometimes blinding compulsion to see our children succeed and live a happy life. Despite all that, I think, in the main, the system works well and that high schools have done a marvelous job of sending student-athletes into the next life phases prepared and ready to roll.

I am, however, a believer in making things better. I believe that if the essential mission of high school sports is to have enduring impact on student-athletes, the path is continuous reassessment, with a willingness to reformulate and reprioritize the core values that define each high school sports program. The reassessment path should be an ongoing priority. It seems difficult to quarrel with that notion, if you believe we have more work to do to better serve our student-athletes. Improvement is always an option, isn't it?

Consider a few queries. What would be the results if each athletic director throughout the nation asked themselves the question, What could

143

my athletic program better do to prepare our student-athletes to become productive citizens and healthy and happy adults? How many do you think would say "nothing"? How many athletic directors and coaches, for example, would answer affirmatively the specific question, Can we do more to get our student-athletes to focus on goal-setting? Or, are we scrupulous enough in paying homage to our communication protocols and stated policies that govern self-advocacy for our student-athletes? How many athletic programs do you think could be more effective in educating student-athletes about nutrition, mindfulness, and wellness? What do you think a survey of coaches would show that asked the question, How often do you teach virtues like empathy and citizenship? How about a survey that called on coaches to quantify how often they sit down with individual players to discuss performance, commitment, and whatever is on their minds? More generally, how often do coaches pay greater homage to the ends of the athletic experience than its means? And to what degree, honestly, do coaches see themselves as teachers and mentors first and coaches second?

*H*igh school sports encase a treasure trove of opportunity for student-athletes to grow.

These sorts of questions, but a sample, are not meant as judgments. Nor are they rhetorical. They are a means to prod and challenge. I know from almost three decades in the coaching ranks that I fell short my share of times. Merely writing this book reminded me of missed opportunities to do more to serve the long-term well-being of my athletes and, in the process, less time I might have devoted to fretting about the win–loss column. The irony, I believe, is that if high schools have highly focused and well-vetted values-based athletic programs that emphasize many, if not all, of the benefits discussed in this book, success by any traditional measure would take care of itself. If anything, teams flourishing in such a culture would overachieve relative to raw talent.

High school sports encase a treasure trove of opportunity for student-athletes to grow emotionally and cognitively, acquire or enhance skills and values that will serve them for all time, and take a major step forward to becoming people who will make us proud no matter what career paths they choose. At their pinnacle, high school sports are more than dress rehearsal for adulthood; they are essential to life, expressed through the cloak of education. As such, they pay tribute to the timeless words of John Dewey: "Education is the process of living, not a preparation for the future of living."[1]

It is all there for the taking. It falls to a constellation of adults, working in harmony, and passionately committed to the task, to make sure the high school sports experience maximizes chances of meeting its broad and special potential. We stand duty bound to be vigilant in improving how we serve our youth. I hope this book contributes in some way toward that end.

High School Sports
Mission Statement

An Exemplar

$\mathscr{T}$he following is one person's vision of an ideal high school sports mission statement. It is offered, as with most everything in this book, in a suggestive spirit, to provoke thought and consideration about the different ways a high school athletic system and culture might be formulated. It is presented without any presumption of wisdom, only a presumption of commitment to improve athletic programs through the community of ideas.

The length of the proposed mission statement is more uncommon than not, as many high school athletic mission statements tend to be a single page or two of succinct bullet points. Taking nothing away from terser formats, for purposes here, an extensive narrative approach is more conducive to incite debate and trigger differing views. It also hopefully engages a wider audience. The hope is that the content will engender opinions and ideas that might otherwise not arise from business as usual. Experience-refined routine is efficient, no question. But it also can stultify. A process of constant reevaluation is what leads to more effective and impactful methods, and in the high school sports context, there can be no greater calling. It is with that sentiment that the following model athletic mission statement is offered, using the hypothetical "Bridge to Futures High School."

ATHLETIC MISSION STATEMENT OF
BRIDGE TO FUTURES HIGH SCHOOL (BTF)

Introduction

We take great pride in the BTF athletic program, which we consider an integral part of our educational process. We are proud, of course, that our sports programs have enjoyed traditions of winning throughout the years and that we have enjoyed success in teaching a wide range of athletic skills, including how to hit a decisive volley in tennis, staunchly defend the goal in lacrosse and soccer, execute a bounce pass that produces a score in basketball, hit a breaking curve in baseball into the gap, run a successful route in football, or hit a game-shattering spike in volleyball. But we are much prouder that every year we teach and mentor our student-athletes well beyond athletic skills, help them acquire the tools and skills to become better citizens and well-rounded people, and prepare them for what awaits them as adults. While championship banners are always in our sight lines and much valued, they are far from the sole barometer of what success means in our athletic program.

We have attempted to ground the athletic program at BTF in a culture that expresses the values and principles we hold important and possesses the resilience to endure. Our experience has taught us that adherence to a value-based athletic system both teaches the many intangibles high school sports have to offer and frees our student-athletes to produce successful seasons according to traditional measures.

We invite our athletes to join us in making the high school sports experience special. We expect student-athletes to work hard, be prepared, and take their roles as high school athletes seriously. High school sports are a significant step up from the athletic challenges they have experienced in the past, and we urge them to greet the new tests with enthusiasm and boldness. For our part, we commit to presenting our athletes with experiences that push them to the edges of their potential and steel them for their future through devotion to the following values and principles.

Our Positivity Culture

It begins with culture. We strive to create an upbeat athletic atmosphere that injects positivity into everything our athletes and their teams do. We value optimism and realism over pessimism. We want a can-do sports environment premised on continuous athletic and personal growth through positive reinforcement. We want to minimize negativity in favor of constructive feedback. We don't shy away from what is difficult and are eager to confront mistake and failure (as discussed later), but above all we want to see our athletes be hopeful and upbeat, to find silver linings in the most trying situations and value what each of them relatively can contribute to their individual sports programs.

We expect our coaches to treat each athlete with respect and take them at their individual skill levels, creating expectations that push the envelope of potential, while at the same time honoring realistic limitations. We want observers of our athletes to marvel about how much fun they have together as they compete with fierce spirit and skill. We want, in short, our coaches and athletes to treat success and failure as positive, interdependent forces that help them feel good for having done what they are capable of doing, enjoy the relationships they have built and, in many cases, will continue to build, and take with them a bright outlook into their futures.

Character

The late Martin Luther King is quoted as saying that the "true" goal of education is "intelligence plus character." It is a perspective we share. At BTF, we ask our coaches to elevate the importance of developing character in our athletes. Identifying moments when character is implicated is a core teaching tool, and we expect our coaching staffs to do their best to bring those lessons to life. We want to model human excellence daily. Our experience is that competitive sports, with all their challenges, distinctively provide opportunities for coaches to identify and nurture exemplary character. The list of character traits a high school sports program can teach is extensive and, among others, includes empathy, compassion, kindness, optimism, respect, self-control, patience, integrity, loyalty, sportsmanship, and fair play.

Challenging the Comfort Zone

The comfort zone, particularly for high school athletes, is a stagnant no-risk, no-failure, and limited-growth isolation haven. BTF demands of its athletes a commitment to do their best to move beyond the coziness of old habits. We want them to leave BTF with new insight into their capabilities and having discovered different ways to express themselves in action. This challenge is especially ripe for student-athletes, for they typically come to high school armed with a wide range of well-entrenched habits from their prior sports life. At BTF, they are presented virtually every day with opportunities and encouragement to overcome those limiting barriers.

Communication

Communication is a separate skill necessary for peak athletic performance. The ability of athletes and coaches to stay in sync depends on how well they communicate, both verbally and nonverbally. Beyond its value as an athletic skill, communication in sports builds team cohesion, respect, and thriving relationships. We want our athletes to become more effective communicators. We want our athletes to talk, share what's on their minds, and be heard. Our coaches are expected to lead the way to ensure effective and positive communication. At

BTF, certain principles of communication are key: candor, open-mindedness, clarity, listening well, thinking before speaking, knowing the audience, and trying to see things as others do.

Community

At BTF, each year we anoint our student-athletes as public ambassadors to cast a positive light on the school in the community. More than any other school activity at BTF, our athletic programs are on public display, and student-athletes are thrust into the role of civic keeper of school values. Our sports program is the ideal vehicle to expose our athletes to multiculturalism and showcase many attributes of our school. We expect our athletes to honor the highest standards of behavior when in public and make proud the school and the communities with which they come in contact.

Confidence and Self-Esteem

Not every athlete can compete at the same level and make the same contributions to their sport. Nonetheless, we value and seek consistently to affirm each athlete at BTF, no matter what sport they choose or role they fill. BTF coaches understand well the profound impact they have on the emotional development and self-esteem of the athletes under their charge and take seriously their roles as leaders and mentors. We want our athletes, as they undergo the major life transition of adolescence, to develop confidence in themselves and a self-image that fuels their drive and makes them feel good about who they are and are becoming.

Conflict Resolution

It is not uncommon for conflicts to arise amid competition in sports, whether in practice or games, between and among teammates, between players and coaches, and in other circumstances. We see conflict as a natural outgrowth of robust competition and a learning opportunity for student-athletes, coaches, and often parents. We emphasize the development of problem-solving skills whenever conflicts arise. In conjunction with communication skills (discussed earlier) and self-advocacy (discussed later), conflict resolution skills are essential to what we seek to develop in our athletes. Our hope is that student-athletes become better equipped to handle tough situations that arise later in their lives.

Decision-Making

Throughout the course of the high school athletic experience, student-athletes will encounter many decision-making opportunities. On a macro level, they might include whether to try out for a specific team or focus exclusively on a single sport or how much to commit to a sport. On a micro level, they principally include how to manage time daily and sometimes whether to attend an event that conflicts with their sport obligations. At BTF, we want our student-athletes, with adult support, to focus on two aspects of decision-making: (1) a process that thoughtfully weighs the relevant and important factors before making a decision and (2) a willingness to accept the consequences of the decisions they make.

Failure and Mistake Response

The late Winston Churchill once said, "Success is stumbling from failure to failure with no loss of enthusiasm." Many have echoed similar sentiments throughout the years, whether pertaining to life generally or athletics specifically. We are firm in our perspective that in athletics, failure is a source of information and learning, and a dynamic entryway to future success. We want our athletes to make mistakes through industrious effort and relentless drive. We take no shame in errors that occur in the halls of keen competition. Each stumble is a call for greater resolve, whether in the next moment of heated competition or when distance provides clarity, to take stock of what went wrong and figure out what can go right the next time. In athletics, we cannot succeed unless we learn to fail well.

Fitness and Wellness

Physical fitness and wellness are essential to athletics on every level, and our sports programs are no different. Our athletic handbook lays out nutritional information, which we update as new information is introduced in health-care sectors. We ask student-athletes and their families to consider the posted nutritional guidelines. More fundamentally, a high school sports program is the ideal situation to develop both a mindset and sound habits about fitness and wellness to last a lifetime. In addition, at BTF we have experimented with yoga and meditation to improve athletic performance and well-being, and expect to expand their use throughout our sports programs. In all, we hope our athletes and families share our commitment to a healthy body and vigorous mind.

Habits and Excellence

One key to success in athletics, as with most aspects of life, is developing sound habits that bring out the best in each athlete. The acquisition and development of good habits often mean breaking down and discarding old habits, and our coaches spend significant time and energy trying to make that happen. Consistency in excellence allows for no less. The challenge is to persuade young athletes to accept the sometimes-prolonged discomfort of the process. Consistency in quality of performance requires courage, patience, commitment to high standards, and the ability to see value in incremental growth on an uncertain timeline. The rewards are many in the short run of a high school athletic career and in the long haul in how student-athletes personally grow.

Perseverance

The high school athletic experience can be an emotional roller-coaster ride, especially when athletes face long odds of success. At one level, we want our athletes and teams to be realistic, for unrealistic expectations are a virtual guarantee of frustration and an undeserved perception of failure. At another level, we value the vitality of hope and seek in our programs to incite belief that our athletes can scale steep mountains in the right circumstances. Beating poor odds of success is one of the wonderful allures of the athletic experience. We don't want our athletes feeling they can't whenever there is room to believe they can. That doesn't mean success follows as a matter of course, only that we strive to teach our athletes to be ambitious, persevere, and be hopeful in whatever they do. Failure comes and goes, but the drive to elevate performance is never-ending.

Goal-Setting

High school sports programs provide extensive opportunities to acquire goal-setting habits, whether on an individual or a team basis, and whether short-term or long-term. We believe that the use of goals improves performance and that goal-setting is an important habit. We want our coaches to work closely with their athletes to develop goal-setting routines they believe serve their athletes and individual sports programs. We have found that setting specific, attainable (meaning realistic) goals that are monitored thoughtfully produces various benefits, among them, improved attitude, self-awareness about strengths and weaknesses, enhanced skills, a sense of success and accomplishment, increased commitment, and more confidence.

Leadership

Leadership is a skill that most every high school athlete can acquire and develop to varying degrees. Some lead with words, some with action, and some with both. We value all styles of leadership. At BTF we have two types of leaders: (1) appointed leaders in the role of captains and (2) emergent leaders in the form of anyone else who wants to assume the mantle of leadership. Our coaches work with captains to define their roles and help them discharge their leadership function effectively. We also expect our coaches to encourage the other athletes to step up and lead in ways in which they are comfortable, supplementing the leadership of their captains.

Mentoring and Role Modeling

Coaches at BTF wear many hats, including as mentor and role model. We want our coaches to guide our athletes through tough times, hear them out, help them make decisions, and nurture their personal and athletic progress on an individual basis. In addition, we expect our coaches to set a high bar for behavior for our athletes to emulate, especially when it comes to character and effective communication. We also want to provide student-athletes opportunities to mentor one another through buddy systems and other methods coaches determine work well, and be role models for other athletes, the student body, and the community.

Self-Discipline

In our experience, athletic performance can suffer when athletes venture outside their control and capacity. We have learned that when athletes and their teams perform within the limits of their capabilities and what they control, they are more successful, happier, and able to grow beyond existing limitations more rapidly. Our coaches endeavor to impose limits on teams and individual players that maximize strengths and minimize weaknesses. That is not to say we don't want our student-athletes to work hard to transform weaknesses into strengths and overcome limitations. We do. It is rather that we strive to take realistic snapshots of skills in given circumstances, urge the exercise of self-discipline within those parameters, and build from there.

Self-Advocacy

One behavior we heavily prize is when student-athletes advocate for themselves. The athletic experience is filled with ups and downs, disappointments and successes, frustration and elation. The emotional power of competition can unsettle at times, and athletes often can be confused or uncertain about their role and sometimes desire a change in their experience. We want our athletes to stand for themselves; to be able to express, without fear of judgment, what is on their minds; and advocate for what they need or believe they have earned.

While desired results, of course, are not guaranteed, taking such initiative holds much promise for long-term empowerment, and we urge each athlete to take charge of their experience as best they are able. Our athletic handbook details the protocols we ask student-athletes and families to honor when situations call for discussion about the athletic experience.

Team Values

Finally, we come to team values, the cornerstone of any athletic program. The first tier of team values important at BTF is team before individual, commitment to the team mission, and acceptance of individual roles. In addition, we honor the values of a strong work ethic, individual discipline, loyalty, integrity, trust, mutual respect, accountability, and honesty. It sounds like a lot to absorb. But we believe each value is displayed in every sport, in different forms, manifesting at different times and sometimes at the same time. We hope our athletes treat those values with utter seriousness because, in the end, they will be what keeps them afloat and energized as they navigate the experience of their sport each year.

Appendix B

Chapter Hypotheticals

$\mathcal{E}$ach chapter has two hypotheticals and follow-up questions designed to provoke thought and debate about the chapter content. While the questions posed might reflect a point of view, the format is not intended to imply any correct answers. On the contrary, the hypotheticals assume there is no right or wrong answers and are intended to trigger proposed solutions specific to how each reader views the described situation. That way, it is hoped, we can stimulate the collective consciousness about matters relevant to high school athletics.

Importantly, as with all hypotheticals, it is not always possible to supply each piece of information a reader might prefer before taking a stand on a presented problem. You might also think there are better questions to ask. Many questions in the drafting process of the hypotheticals fell to the cutting-room floor in favor of limiting their number. Augment as you deem fit. The hypotheticals are a reader exercise, and supplementing the facts to make problems more applicable and adding questions to make the exercise more meaningful is quite useful. Determine what more specifically is needed and ruminate on how you might handle the situation given the different factors. And if moved even more, present the hypothetical situation to others to stimulate debate and create a community of ideas, which is the ideal situation for maximizing the value of this process.

A diversified readership also means different perspectives on the hypotheticals. The hypotheticals are not one-size-fits-all problems, and you might want to skip some that don't apply to you. Still, the following are some comments to help broaden application.

If you are a coach, for example, depending on the sport you teach, you might not think each situation applies directly to you. For the purposes of this exercise, try to assume it does and, again, fill in perceived blanks necessary for the hypothetical to be more applicable to you. If you are an athletic director, unless it is an athletic director question, consider how you might advise a coach who brings the problem to you to vet or how you might otherwise handle it as a coach. If you are a parent, consider how you hope a coach of your children or athletic director at your school might handle the situation. If you wear another hat, for instance, an athlete, community member, fan, or member of the media, consider the hypothetical a platform to formulate and express your views on the assumption you are told your input is valued and wanted.

CHAPTER 1: CRITICISM OF HIGH SCHOOL ATHLETICS

Hypothetical No. 1

Your most talented athlete asks for a private meeting. He explains his father is intent on pulling him from the high school in favor of homeschooling so he can concentrate more on his athletic ability to increase chances of a college career and possibly the professional ranks. He tells you he is torn about what to do. He told his dad he intended to seek you out.

1. What is your immediate (and private) reaction and with whom, if anyone, do you share it?
2. Generally, what approach will you take to facilitate the discussion?
3. What specific factors will you offer the athlete to consider and with what relative emphasis?
4. If he asks directly, will you give him your opinion of homeschooling generally and specifically as a means to build a long-term athletic career, and even if he doesn't, will you offer it anyway, and why?

Hypothetical No. 2

You are the athletic director at a high school and receive a compilation of complaints about parental behavior in games, home and away: heckling opposing players, giving instructions to their children during competition, and complaining about coaching decisions and referee calls. This behavior seems ingrained, as it occurs habitually.

1. Do you attack this problem directly with individual parents or let it go because it is too difficult to craft solutions on a person-by-person basis, which is what you believe may be needed?

2. If you are committed to changing the behavior, what are your options other than one-on-one discussions with the implicated parents to get your point across? Announcements before games? Written messages or memos to the parents at the school? Address the issues when parents of athletes are gathered for other purposes? Other acceptable approaches?
3. If parents persist in conduct you find unacceptable after you have tried to remedy things, what action, if any, do you take?
4. How do you handle the impact of the behavior on your players in terms of role modeling and values?

CHAPTER 2: SELF-ADVOCACY

Hypothetical No. 1

One of your players seems unhappy about her role on the team. She broods often and is withdrawn. Before you can intervene, you receive an e-mail from her mother asking for a meeting to discuss her "daughter's role and treatment on the team." The school and you have a rule about protocol in this situation: The player, without parent, is expected to approach the head coach first, and if that doesn't bring resolution, the player can ask for a meeting with the athletic director, during which time parents may attend. Additionally, you learn that this parent is actively involved in all aspects of her daughter's life, some referring to her, pejoratively, as a "helicopter parent." You respond to the mother, reminding her of the protocol, and she writes back demanding a meeting immediately.

1. Do you toss protocol aside and meet with the parent alone to gather information and use the opportunity to open her to the importance of self-advocacy?
2. If you meet privately with her, how would you handle matters if the parent demands that you not tell her daughter the two of you met?
3. Do you, instead, refuse to meet, insisting the player come to you without any adult?
4. Do you agree to meet so long as the player is present in the hope of using the opportunity to impart lessons to both player and parent about self-advocacy?

Hypothetical No. 2

You have begun a new job as head coach of a varsity team and are eager to introduce a new defensive system you used in other high school programs, with success. It can be a little complicated depending on the sports IQ of the athletes, but once it is nailed down, it's effective, although some teams acclimate to the system more quickly than others. In this case, it's a slow go. You are hesitant to force something on them without buy-in or that doesn't fit them as athletes. At the same time, you worry that the initial struggle is nothing more than a comfort-level dynamic. No one is speaking up about it, but precious practice time is absorbed for something that might not work.

1. Do you wait for your captains or someone else to speak up, and how long do you wait?
2. Do you call a team meeting and give players the opportunity to share how they feel about the system?
3. If you elect to speak with captains only, do you follow up with a team meeting?
4. Regardless of the steps taken to address the problem, how do you make sure the lessons of initiative are nurtured and don't get lost in the shuffle?

CHAPTER 3: LEVERAGING MISTAKES AND FAILURE

Hypothetical No. 1

You have taken over a basketball program with a history of losing records. Your initial program-building focus is to change the culture so your athletes believe in themselves and their ability to complete at the league level and beyond. You are off to a good start, with a winning record guaranteed this season, and if you win your final league game, the team will qualify for league playoffs for the first time in more than a decade. As the game winds down in the fourth quarter, the boys are about to clinch the win and a playoff berth. Then this happens: With less than 40 seconds left, your team has the ball, up three points. Although the team fails to convert the possession, on the ensuing rebound, the opposing center violently tosses your center to the ground and gets called for a technical, which means your team is awarded two shots and possession of the ball. The game seems a lock. You can go up five and get the ball back. While the players on the ground are getting up, however, one of your players on the floor runs at the opposing center and pushes him hard in the chest in retaliation and is called for his own technical. Because the officials deem the technical-generating incidents independent of one another, they are not offsetting, meaning both teams get to shoot two foul shots, and the other team gets awarded possession of the ball after all foul shots are taken. Your team misses both shots, while the other team makes both of theirs—making it a one-point game—and then after holding the ball for most of the shot clock on the ensuing awarded possession, they score at the other end with less than five seconds left to win by one. A program-changing moment is lost because one of your players made an egregious mistake.

1. Do you pull the erring player aside before the postgame meeting to discuss the situation, and if you do, what is the message?
2. If not, do you address the situation with the entire team in the post-game locker room meeting, and if you do, what's that message?
3. If you decide to let the dust settle until the next day, how do you handle the situation?
4. What are your personal challenges here as coach and teacher, and what are the lessons about mistake response?

Hypothetical No. 2

The most talented player in your program struggles to understand the basics of your offensive and defensive systems. In school, he has diagnosed learning differences, which carry over to his inability to grasp what the team is doing. He consistently seems lost in games, missing assignments regularly, although, from time to time, he contributes with spectacular plays, operating in his own private universe. If he were most anyone else on the team, you would pull him off the floor more often because of his lack of team connectiveness. You manage his minutes because of the mistakes but feel frustrated because he has so much raw talent and loves the game intensely. Your team is supportive of him generally but gets annoyed, sometimes with you, when his mistakes pile up during games and you let it go. You don't want to discourage him, and you don't want your players to feel you are favoring him unfairly.

1. Who do you confer with at the school to get a bigger picture of the athlete's situation?
2. Do you apply a separate standard to him and pick your spots more carefully with him?
3. How could you use teammates to help with the situation?
4. What is the most effective way to teach him—and the team in the process—the value of good mistake response, while maintaining the integrity of standards for expectations for all players?

CHAPTER 4: GOAL-SETTING

Hypothetical No. 1

You want each of the players in your program, at every level—varsity, junior varsity, freshman, or freshman-sophomore—to adopt a form of goal-setting each year and have it become an integral part of the culture you are building. You call a meeting of all coaches in your program—head and assistant—to work out the details of what to put together. During the meeting several questions arise, including the following:

1. How is accountability assured in the process?
2. Should coaches each have their own goals, both individually and for the respective teams, to set an example, and if so, to what extent should the coaches share them with the teams?
3. What can be done to ensure individual goals are realistic, and how do coaches handle unrealistic goals?
4. How often should coaches meet with individual players to discuss goal progress, and how do coaches use incremental progress to bolster confidence and define success?

Hypothetical No. 2

After asking each player to set short-term and long-term goals for themselves, your assistant coach tells you one player can't formulate meaningful benchmarks for herself. She is a good athlete, but her drive is sometimes less than mountain-moving, which you attribute to her confidence vacuum. Realistically, you fear that if left to her own devices, she will pass through the year without specific goals to chase and, in the end, be unhappy with the results, which may deplete her motivation further.

1. Do you give her the space to fumble around for a while to figure out a goal-setting plan for herself to see what that brings?
2. Or, do you instead suggest goals you believe are realistic and try to get her buy-in on them?
3. Do you monitor her more closely than the others, and how do you get her confidence to rise?
4. Do you pair her with a teammate to provide ballast and support?

CHAPTER 5: CONQUERING THE COMFORT ZONE

Hypothetical No. 1

You believe a particular skill is essential to maximizing team success and, as a result, relentlessly emphasize it in drills each practice. For whatever reasons, however, in this instance, most of your athletes don't transfer what they hone in practice to game situations. After a while, you are convinced you are facing a collective comfort zone phenomenon. You are, however, unwilling to give it up, believing that if your players transform this skill into habit, it will make a tangible difference in game performance and even outcomes.

1. Do you canvass individual players to get a better feel for the problem?
2. Should you convene a team meeting to discuss what seems to be a collective blockage in executing the skill, and if so, what are the meeting goals?
3. Can you think of an appropriate reward system to benefit players who execute the skill successfully in game situations, and if so, is the reward applicable only if the skill produces a good result or will a mere attempt to execute earn it?
4. Should there be punishment for failing to do so, like coming out of the game? Is that ever appropriate, and if so, in what circumstances?

Hypothetical No. 2

Among all your practice peeves, the most prominent is getting players to take major strides outside the boundaries of their respective comfort zones and conquer individual fears. Each practice you devote substantial energy and focus to urging your athletes to challenge themselves in this respect, with less-than-desirable results, as ingrained habits seem impenetrable. You sense that the problem may be that you are dictating too much—in other words, your approach may include too much top-down, external motivation—and you may be better off making each player responsible for how best to overcome internal resistance to change.

1. How do you present the challenge to the team generally, keeping in mind your goal to empower them to control the process of overcoming their personal comfort zones?

2. What is the most effective way to get each player to identify their greatest areas of resistance and fears regarding skill development and competitive performance, for example, do you ask each player to compile a short list, do you hold a meeting to discuss the matter candidly among the team, do you meet individually with each player, or do you do something else?
3. To what extent, if at all, do you see value in asking players to discuss their comfortable habits outside of school to make the experience more impactful and personal?
4. Once areas of resistance are identified—for example, the fear of physical contact in competition—how do you construct a system that holds each player accountable for the changes they concede they need to make?

CHAPTER 6: THE POWER OF TEAM

Hypothetical No. 1

Your varsity team has talent and is playing relatively well. Still, the coaching staff, you included, believe they are not playing as well as they are capable, owing in the main to a lack of cohesive teamwork. All the barking in practice about working together is not producing the results you want, and you are convinced you need to try something else. You decide to hold a team meeting to discuss the power of team.

1. What team qualities do you want to discuss, and how in the meeting do you get them identified and described?
2. Similarly, what behaviors that undermine good teamwork do you want to highlight, and how do you get them identified and described?
3. How can you use game and practice film to illustrate the differences between the two?
4. What other ways are available to you, relative to the program and culture, for instance, a team bowling outing or movie night, different ways to structure practices or internal scrimmages, team dinners, and so on, to impress upon your athletes the power of team and improve cohesion?

Hypothetical No. 2

It doesn't take long after the start of the season to see you might have a major team problem, as a few players seem more interested in themselves than the team and tend to be divisive. To make matters worse, they have formed a cabal to militate against other teammates whose roles on the team they covet. You wait to see how it plays out for a short while, but nothing changes; the writing is on the wall. You have no team cohesion, a situation teeming with jealousy and an unseemly internal power struggle. In the absence of a solution, the team faces a calamitous season.

1. Because of potential political problems, do you consult with your athletic director (AD) about what to do, and what action do you recommend to the AD be taken?
2. Do you meet separately with each of the wayward players, and if so, what is the agenda and goals of the meeting?
3. Do you, regardless of individual meetings, meet with the team as a group to hash it all out, again with what agenda and goals?
4. What can you do outside of holding meetings to improve the situation?

CHAPTER 7: LEADERSHIP

Hypothetical No. 1

Your school has a strict, nonnegotiable policy that teams (and not coaches) determine their captains through a process coaches may fashion. You are not happy about the policy but must follow it. You believe in strong leadership on your team and are concerned about implementing the policy this year because of the risk that popular or senior players lacking in leadership skills might get the nod.

1. Because you have discretion to determine process, do you provide the team with a list of criteria to govern their selections, and if so, what would it include?
2. How can you make players accountable in using the criteria? Should your list of criteria not only exclude popularity or year at the school, but also expressly forbid reliance on those factors?
3. Should you ask players who want consideration as captains to both identify themselves so the team has a slate of candidates and demonstrate through some means, for example, a presentation, why they are suitable for the role?
4. What other means are available to ensure the quality of the process and minimize the chances the team will elect someone without leadership skills?

Hypothetical No. 2

You have several players on your team, in addition to elected captains, who possess leadership qualities and are committed to developing leadership skills in as many of your athletes as possible.

1. Should you meet with each noncaptain to discuss ways they can provide team leadership, and what would you discuss with them?
2. Are there outer bounds of captain responsibilities that should determine where the roles of emergent leaders should begin, and if so, what are they?
3. How can you maximize leadership contributions from noncaptains?
4. To what extent do you give noncaptains the freedom to undertake leadership when they are comfortable doing so?

CHAPTER 8: CITIZENSHIP AND COMMUNITY

Hypothetical No. 1

The head of your high school announces she wants each athletic program to make community-building and awareness a priority this season and each season going forward. She believes community fabrics are undergoing rupture and high schools have a unique opportunity to become vehicles of change: "Our sports teams are often in the public eye and well-positioned to both teach our student-athletes the importance of community in their lives and become carriers of sound community values." Of keen importance, she stresses, is understanding the "differences in communities and cultures." She calls on coaches to gather within each program to elevate community based on the list of coaching priorities. You meet with your coaching staff to discuss the new policy.

1. In implementing the newly stated policy, what specific qualities of community do you want your players to experience and advance?
2. Your staff suggests creating a prioritized list of at least five community activities outside of customary school sport activities. What would be on the list and in what order?
3. How might you make effective use of the community activities in which your athletes and their families already participate?
4. How can you use parents as a resource in implementing the new policy?

Hypothetical No. 2

Your public-school team is ethnically and religiously diverse. You notice that while everyone seems to get along, when you ask the team to work in pairs in practice for various drills, their default for pairing up is ethnic or religious identity. The same stratification pertains on campus as well, in larger groups, of course, although you aren't sure that is a bad thing, as it provides a sense of belonging. In any event, there is an opportunity to raise consciousness about other cultures within the confines of team relationships.

1. What steps can you take to take advantage of the opportunity?
2. If you held a team meeting to discuss diversity, how would you present and organize the dialogue?
3. What are the advantages and disadvantages of involving parents in this process, and when and how, if at all, do you include them? Similarly, how might you involve classroom teaching staff?
4. What possible use at the school beyond your sports program can you make of whatever results this effort generates?

CHAPTER 9: SELF-ESTEEM AND CONFIDENCE

Hypothetical No. 1

One criticism of your coaching style, as recounted in player evaluations after the previous year, is that you are too tough on players and confuse tough love with being plain tough. One player anonymously wrote, "While coach knows her stuff and we learn a ton, the old-school technique drained me to the point where I couldn't imagine doing anything right." You found the evaluation surprising, as it didn't comport with your self-perception, and as a result, it got in your craw. Your athletic director sits down with you to discuss style and the fragile egos of players in high school. It is a wake-up call, and you know you should modify your style.

1. What personal changes can you entertain to improve your mentoring function, and what role can your coaching staff play in this process?
2. What sources of information can you tap to get a better handle on the internal workings of your athletes?
3. What specific things might you do on a player-by-player basis to ensure a better job of building and nurturing self-esteem?

4. How can you better handle difficult personalities who, on the surface, don't accept your personal and direct commentary, positive or constructive?

Hypothetical No. 2

Your most talented athlete, interestingly, probably has the lowest self-esteem on the team. The gulf between her talent and self-image is like nothing you've experienced as a coach. In games, she is generally fine. She is skilled; she gets it done. But she and you both know she has more to offer and isn't happy because she doesn't see herself positively. She never seems satisfied with her performance. You want to extend yourself to help improve her self-esteem before she moves on past high school.

1. What roles can her parents, teachers, and administrators at the school play to assist you?
2. Do you meet with her, and if so, what is the focus of the discussion?
3. What specific things can you do to help her on the path to a better internal sense of self?
4. How specific should your affirmations of her be, as opposed to generic comments, for instance, about jobs well done?

CHAPTER 10: THE PURSUIT OF CONSISTENCY IN EXCELLENCE

Hypothetical No. 1

Your team has more than its share of poor habits, which threaten to undermine the standards you have set to achieve consistently high-level performance. Players have talent, but you fear they will underachieve without developed routines that refine their skills. In fairness, prior coaching staffs were not big on emphasizing a regime of working on skills and conditioning outside the realm of team activities. While you don't want to overload them, players keep talking the talk about achieving great things, words that ring hollow without a commensurate effort and genuine commitment to make that happen. You are focused on the development of good habits.

1. What specific things can you say and do to help your players appreciate how good habits lead to consistency in performance excellence?

2. What can you do for your players to see the converse, that is, how bad habits produce bad results and undermine long-term goals?
3. What are the pros and cons of filming practice for this purpose?
4. Can you imagine any practical way to chart habit growth or at least hold players accountable for working on good habits?

Hypothetical No. 2

You decide this season to take a different approach regarding the development of good habits, one more in line with the traditional classroom. You will have players, in small groups, research what successful college, professional, and Olympic athletes, regardless of sport, have identified as their most effective habits. Your coaching staff will work with the groups to help guide the research and compile the results.

1. What is the first thing to do once the research results are compiled?
2. After that, what are the different ways to make effective use of the research results for the team?
3. How can you use this process to build team camaraderie and increase the investment each player has in the team?
4. Are there effective ways to construct a reward system based on the research results?

CHAPTER 11: THE POWER OF LIMITS

Hypothetical No. 1

Like many coaches, you preach the importance of controlling what your players can control and not trying to control what they can't. You have not, however, imposed any formal system to implement that principle, particularly as it relates to skills and performance, and as you enter a new season, you decide to give it a shot. Your thought is to impose strict team-wide limitations on what each player may do in games to maximize efficiency of performance and success.

1. How do you describe to your athletes the importance of the new system to get buy-in, considering the sensibilities of your athletes, including egos?
2. What process do you employ to specify the strengths and weaknesses of your athletes and thus what is and is not off limits?

3. How do you handle differences of view between coaches and players in terms of skill readiness and impose limits while helping players transcend those limits?
4. What kinds of self-evaluation mechanisms are available for players as part of this limitations program?

Hypothetical No. 2

Your coaching style prefers giving teams leeway to call plays and sets and run the offense with relatively limited coaching control. When you have a senior-laden team it tends to work well enough, but this year you have a young corps of athletes and their decision-making leaves much to be desired. You don't want to handcuff them too much but are quickly concluding they need limits imposed on them to improve and be effective.

1. How do you explain the value of the coach-controlled limitations while encouraging their growth as a unit?
2. To what extent would you permit the team to have a say in what limitations to impose?
3. To what extent might the limitations include automatic playing time restrictions for players who have a propensity to become sloppy or inefficient after certain stretches of time, for instance, two minutes and out of the game?
4. In what circumstances would you consider lifting or scaling back the restrictions?

CHAPTER 12: EFFECTIVE COMMUNICATION

Hypothetical No. 1

You have a sophomore who is a rising star. You make him a starter, a role he deserves and is in the best long-term interest of the team. He is quiet and unassuming, loves the game, and goes about his business in a workmanlike and respectful manner. You notice behavior in some older players, however, especially players whose minutes he has garnered, who seem to shun him in practice. You also get a sense he is sometimes frozen out in games. He hasn't complained or shown ill effects from this presumed treatment, but on the other hand, he is ill-disposed to rock boats and it's hard to know what he is feeling. You are not entirely sure about what you think you see and entertain the possibility you are reading into it too much. But when you mention it to the rest of your staff, they agree. It could all go away throughout time. It could also become a cancer. You decide to address it.

1. What kind of communication path do you follow—individual, group, or team—and in what combinations and why?
2. What do you present as the subject matter, and what are your discussion goals?
3. What role do coaches play in the discussions?
4. What rules and principles of communication do you want the discussions to feature?

Hypothetical No. 2

Your attempts to have team meetings to watch game film have been met with mixed success. The main problem is attention span. Your players are usually good for 20, maybe 30 minutes on a good day, after which they devolve into silly chatter and fidgeting. You can accept their attention limitations but are not prepared to dispense with the value of game film. You decide to require them to watch game film on their own, after which they are expected to present their critical observations in a group format. You create groups and assign aspects of games for this purpose. Each group is required to make a 5- to 10-minute presentation on specific strengths and weaknesses, mistakes, and areas of improvement within the parameters of what you assign, and each group member is expected to participate in the presentation, like a panel. If practical, you assign an assistant and yourself to each group to guide the process.

1. How do you determine group composition, for example, based on speaking skills, team roles or positions, school class, or something else? What is your thinking here?
2. Do you keep the groups the same or alter them as the season goes on?
3. What preparation, communication, and presentation guidelines do you give them, that is, how to give constructive feedback based on what they see on the film?
4. Once a presentation is completed, what audience participation do you permit, for example, does the rest of the team get to ask questions of the presenters or critique the presentations?

CHAPTER 13: DECISION-MAKING

Hypothetical No. 1

The prior season, a transfer student, a junior, came out for your varsity team. He made the team and quickly became an effective and welcome addition, contributing in many ways. Remarkably, he hadn't played the sport prior to high school but is an incredible athlete. He has huge potential and works in the summer to improve. As the current season approaches, however, he expresses doubt about whether he wants to play again, intimating he lacks "passion" for the sport. You'd hate to lose him. He provides a needed dimension, and his teammates respect and want him back. On the other hand, you have committed to keeping a specific number of players and would hate to see him take up a spot that someone else might fill with more commitment and love for the game, albeit with less talent. Fortunately, he contacts you as tryouts approach to discuss the situation.

1. What is your thinking about who should attend the meeting? Should it, for example, be restricted to the two of you?
2. What are the factors—the pros and cons—you think he should consider in making his decision?
3. What is the most effective way to ensure he fairly considers and weighs those factors?
4. What concrete guidance can you offer him to assist in the decision-making process, including what questions you might ask him to facilitate the thought process?

Hypothetical No. 2

A national movement, most evident at the professional level of sports, has erupted where athletes are "taking a knee" during the playing of the national anthem before the start of games as a form of political protest. Your captains approach you before practice one day and say team members have discussed providing support for the movement by taking a knee during the anthem before upcoming games. Rather than proceed with that limited information, you decide to hold a team meeting to facilitate thoughtful decision-making.

1. Should you first confer with your athletic director before the meeting, and if so, toward what end?
2. What decisional paths are available for athletes who want to take a public stand if the school forbids the proposed conduct?
3. How can the coaches best assist the team and individuals in making informed decisions about how to express themselves, including factors to consider and ultimate goals?
4. How do you guard against peer pressure in this setting and the potential tension between players taking different approaches to what can be an emotional and divisive subject?

CHAPTER 14: HOPE AND BELIEF:
THE ELIXIR OF ATHLETIC COMPETITION

Hypothetical No. 1

Your team makes an astonishing and improbable comeback in a league game, an experience that shakes heads, gives your players an injection of confidence, and thrills everyone connected with your program. It is memorable. It also provides an opportunity for a major lesson about hope and belief (and perseverance), and rather than leave the experience to an engraved and exhilarating sports memory, you want your athletes to gain something about the power of having belief in what they can achieve and how it applies to most everything they will do in life. You decide to sacrifice some practice time the next day to explore the matter.

1. What format do you use for the discussion, and how do you present the subject matter?
2. What do you say about hope and what do you say about belief?
3. How do you get normally reticent players to chime in?
4. What use do you make of the results of the meeting?

Hypothetical No. 2

You want to teach your players about the power of hope and belief outside the arena of athletics to help them more effectively incorporate what they learn from athletic performance. Although you are concerned about taking too much time outside of practice and games, you think it is important to expose them to perspectives outside the world they inhabit as high school athletes.

1. What are the pros and cons of bringing in an inspirational speaker, and if you do, do you invite others, for instance, parents, and how would you use the results of the speaking experience?
2. Do you provide them instead tailored, short-reading material to discuss, and again, do you hold a meeting to share impressions?
3. What are the pros and cons of a routine of watching select "underdog" or against-the-odds films before select games to help drive their motivation and boost their confidence, perhaps as part of a pregame dinner?
4. What other options for teaching here are available to you?

CHAPTER 15: CONFLICT RESOLUTION

Hypothetical No. 1

You kept one starting position competitively open hoping to inspire the two candidates for the role to raise their game. To that extent, you were correct. Both players have answered the bell, working hard to distinguish themselves. Unfortunately, the good news came with a flip side: Their maturity levels have led to severe conflicts between them in practice, which, while expected to some extent, you presumed would pass as normal initial pains of the process. They haven't passed, and in one memorable practice, they almost came to blows and had to be separated by teammates. You now have a full-fledged problem on your hands that threatens team chemistry and could breed bitterness in the two athletes. But you also see opportunity here, for if this conflict can be solved well, it could set a standard for how teammates deal with one another and resolve differences.

1. What are the pros and cons of meeting options, for example, separate meetings between each player and coaches, a meeting between the two players with coaches present to facilitate, or other?
2. Is there merit in involving other members of the team, say captains, in some capacity, and what role should coaches play in any discussions?
3. How do you present the subject of the meeting and its goals, and what guidance or tools do you provide the players to help them get their feelings out and see one another's perspectives?
4. What other things can you do, postmeeting, to reinforce lessons learned and affirm the courage of the two players to resolve their differences, and what do you do if this process doesn't produce a positive outcome?

Hypothetical No. 2

One of your players is young, brash, and immature. If she is not the most talented player on the team, she will be by the end of the season. She has a promising high school athletic career ahead of her. She sometimes dogs it in practice, however, and you learn through the grapevine that she sometimes makes derogatory comments about you and the other coaches, and regularly trash talks teammates. Eventually, the captains approach you to express their concerns, informing you that many on the team are frustrated with her and that the situation, in their judgment, has ripened into a significant problem.

While you have seen a slice of the behavior, you are concerned about proceeding based on anecdotal information but know you must act.

1. What do you see as the sequence of meetings here, for example, the player first (alone or with others), with the captains to get their full perspective and input on how to handle, with teammates to get more concrete information, with your AD, and so on?
2. What merit do you see in conferring confidentially with other adults in her life, including school personnel, to gain insight?
3. When you speak to her in the process, how do you present the problem and what do you want to gain from her?
4. What are you seeking to accomplish overall?

CHAPTER 16: CHARACTER

Hypothetical No. 1

You are head coach of the boys' varsity basketball team. One of your players has an uncanny long-range shot. It identifies him. Early in the season, he suffers a mild shooting slump, and the coaches encourage him to keep shooting, which of course he does. During an early season tournament game, he hits stride, gets in a zone, and starts draining consecutive three-point shots. After each make, however, he does something you've never seen him do before: He stares down his defender as he backpedals to play defense and flashes three fingers high in the air. This behavior doesn't go unnoticed in the gym, and the opposing team's fans start to heckle him. Still, he continues to make shots and display the postmake one-upmanship. You decide not to say anything during the game in favor of a better opportunity to address the behavior, which you find unacceptable.

1. From a teaching standpoint, which values implicated in the behavior are you inclined to highlight and address?
2. Do you meet with him without the team to discuss the conduct, and if so, how do you teach him the life lesson without putting a damper on the confidence he rediscovered during that game?
3. Do you discuss the behavior with the team at some point, and if so, how do you present the issues, and what benefits, if any, do you see in having him address the team about what happened and what he may have learned?

4. In the team setting, how do you protect against singling him out too critically for inappropriate behavior while advancing lessons about character-based values?

Hypothetical No. 2

After the season has wound down, as the postseason team party approaches, you decide to step outside tradition. Instead of you doing the lion's share of the talking at the postseason gathering, you decide to share the stage with the players by having them present to the assembly of teammates and family members. Your idea is to have each teammate speak for less than one minute about one other teammate, focusing exclusively on an admirable character trait the speaker believes the teammate possesses.

1. Do you provide the team a list of nonexclusive character traits to get them focused, and if so, what's on the list?
2. Do you meet with players one-on-one in advance to help them put their presentations together or leave them to their own devices?
3. What guidance do you give to get them comfortable with presentation dynamics, knowing not every athlete will be at ease delivering words in front of teammates and their families?
4. What criteria do you use to assign teammates?

CHAPTER 17: LEARNING THE IMPORTANCE OF MENTORS AND ROLE MODELS

Hypothetical No. 1

You decide as the season approaches to stress the benefits of role models within the confines of team activities. Part of your motivation is to redefine behavioral standards and expectations, especially regarding the intangible benefits of your program. Your initial thought is to have coaches routinely call out and commend behavior that stands out as role model material, whenever and wherever it occurs.

1. Do you ask the team to identify the behavioral traits they admire most in others (and why), do the coaches instead create a list, or do you play it by ear and merely identify the valued behavior as it occurs during the season?
2. Regardless of how you organize your efforts, and assuming you compile a list of identified behaviors during the season, what use can you make of the list down the road?

3. How do you handle behaviors that shouldn't be modeled?
4. What role, if any, should your AD or parents play in this process?

Hypothetical No. 2

You have had success with buddy systems and other ways to create a mentoring culture in your sports programs. High school students, in your experience, seem eager to learn how to teach others and take pride in doing so. Now you want to try something different. You want your players each to experience the mentor role by working with less-fortunate kids in the local community. You know organizations exist in the community that would welcome involvement of your team in some capacity.

1. Where do you start once you account for any school-dictated restrictions?
2. How do you describe the nature, purpose, and goals of this effort to your athletes, and what guidelines, rules, and restrictions do you provide them?
3. What roles do you see for parents on this project?
4. At some point, individual players will work with individual kids in the community in some capacity. What criteria do you use to assign players to kids in the community?

CHAPTER 18: HEALTH AND WELLNESS

Hypothetical No. 1

You have seen what your players tend to eat when on their own. You know that getting them to change eating habits is a major comfort zone challenge, and you harbor doubts you will succeed. Given the ambitious nature of your athletic program, you are concerned with picking your spots. Still, you believe sound nutrition is important for them as athletes and, more importantly, as a lifelong habit. You also know that, to some extent, this is one of those areas where coaching and parenting overlap, and you assume parents will largely support an effort to get their children to eat better.

1. How do you structure and organize the nutritional program?
2. What sources of information and knowledgeable personnel do you consult?
3. What is the most effective way to present the benefits of nutrition and balanced eating to the players?

4. What monitoring system options are available, including tracking weight and body fat?

Hypothetical No. 2

Mindfulness training and meditation have become a trend among professional athletes, and you are intrigued by how they might enhance athletic performance and improve personal well-being. You decide to introduce meditation practice to your athletes. To make it easier for your players to embrace, your clever idea is to add meditation as the kickoff activity to weekly (and required) weight training before practice. You want the program to be long-term and continue beyond the regular season of your sport.

1. How do you introduce the purpose and benefits of meditation and sell your players on the value of mindfulness, both in athletics and their lives?
2. Do you include videos or testimonials from popular professional athletes on meditation practice and/or bring in a meditation professional to assist in describing the benefits and techniques?
3. Do you see value in having the coaching staff participate in the meditation portion of the weight training to set an example?
4. How will you assess the success of meditation practice?

CHAPTER 19: THE POSITIVITY CULTURE

Hypothetical No. 1

You knew in the back of your mind that the upcoming game could get ugly, and in hindsight, as game time approaches, you feel swells of regret that you added the game to the preleague schedule. Your original thought was the team could use at least one game to expose them to first-tier talent and held the possibility of a major boost in confidence if they could rise to the occasion with a competitive showing, win or lose. That is why you scheduled the game near the end of the preleague part of the season, with league competition around the corner. Unfortunately, the team has not evolved as you hoped, and midway through the contest, no doubt exists that the team is in the throes of a classic blowout. There is no chance of winning or even teasing a bolt of confidence based on the way things are going. Your job is to find ways to produce positive feelings.

1. What adjustments can you make to create small successes to bolster the confidence of your athletes?

2. Do you give any attention to the scoreboard at this point?
3. What are the team goals going forward?
4. What messages do you want your players to receive from this experience?

Hypothetical No. 2

You take over a sports program historically marred with underachievement. Some derisively refer to the program as the "losing culture." The expectations from the community are muted somewhat, owing to the history, but everyone still wants to see higher numbers in the wins column. Simply put, they want what most communities want: a winning program. You see the early goings as a rebuilding process and less about wins and losses and more about creating an enduring atmosphere where athletes feel good, positive, and proud to compete. The wins, you feel, can come next. Thus, you see the short-term goal as ridding the culture of negativity. On the other hand, if the win–loss ratio doesn't improve substantially, you risk getting booted from the job before you can give life to your vision.

1. What positive attitudes, beliefs, and attitudes do you want your program to represent?
2. How do you describe your overall vision to the athletic director, your athletes, coaching staff, and parents in a way that gets buy-in from them?
3. What can you do with daily practices to bolster belief and confidence, and create a positive environment?
4. What else can you do program-wise to create a positive culture considering the history?

Notes

PREFACE

1. Jessica Marati, "30 Motivational Quotes from the Sports World," *Ecosalon*, March 6, 2012, http://ecosalon.com/30-motivational-quotes-from-the-sports-world.

INTRODUCTION

1. Doug Samuels, "Next Time You're Asked, 'What Do You Think of Your Team?' Reflect on This Response from a Hall of Fame Head Coach," *Football Scoop*, June 23, 2016, http://footballscoop.com/news/next-time-youre-asked-think-team -consider-response-hall-fame-head-coach/.

2. John E. Tufte, *Crazy-Proofing High School Sports* (Lanham, MD: Rowman & Littlefield, 2012), 2.

CHAPTER 1

1. This scenario is derived from an interview by the author of a former high school athlete. Each of the remaining book scenarios that introduce chapters are based on the author's personal coaching experience.

2. Amanda Ripley, "The Case against High School Athletics," *Atlantic*, October 2013, www.theatlantic.com/magazine/archive/2013/10/the-case-against-high -school-sports/309447/.

3. Mike Honda, "Why American Students Lag Behind," *CNN*, December 17, 2010, www.cnn.com/2010/OPINION/12/17/honda.education/index.html.

4. Edward B. Fiske and *International Herald Tribune*, "Insights into Why U.S. Students Lag behind in Global Academic 'Horse Race,'" *New York Times*, February 11, 1997, www.nytimes.com/1997/02/11/news/insights-into-why-us-students-lag-behind-in-global-academic-horse-race.html.

5. Corporation for National Community Service, "Community Service and Service-Learning in America's Schools," *Corporation for National Community Service*, November 2008, www.nationalservice.gov/pdf/08_1112_lsa_prevalence.pdf.

6. Daniel H. Bowen and Jay P. Greene, "Does Athletic Success Come at the Expense of Academic Success?" *Journal of Research in Education*, 22, no. 2 (Fall 2012): 1.

7. Bowen and Greene, "Does Athletic Success Come at the Expense of Academic Success?," 1–2.

8. John E. Tufte, *Crazy-Proofing High School Sports* (Lanham, MD: Rowman & Littlefield, 2012), 119.

9. Ripley, "The Case against High School Athletics."

10. "William S. Burroughs Quotes," *BrainyQuote*, www.brainyquote.com/quotes/quotes/w/williamsb383613.html.

11. National Federation of State High School Associations, "The Case for High School Activities," *Massachusetts Interscholastic Athletic Association*, 2014, www.miaa.net/gen/miaa_generated_bin/documents/basic_module/case_for_highschool_activities.pdf, 1, 2.

12. Juli Doshan, "Why We Play: The Purpose of Education-Based Athletics," *National Federation of State High School Associations*, February 11, 2015, www.nfhs.org/articles/why-we-play-the-purpose-of-education-based-athletics/.

13. Ripley, "The Case against High School Athletics."

14. See, for example, National Federation of State High School Associations, "The Case for High School Activities" (studies collected), *National Federation of State High School Associations*, 2017, www.nfhs.org/articles/the-case-for-high-school-activities/; "The Benefits of an Interscholastic Athletic Program" (studies collected), *Lockport City School District*, www.section6.e1b.org/cms/lib/NY19000854/Centricity/shared/ad_tool_kit/BenefitsofAthleticsBrochure.pdf; Heather J. Clark, Martin Camiré, Terrance J. Wade, and John Cairney, "Sport Participation and Its Association with Social and Psychological Factors Known to Predict Substance Use and Abuse among Youth: A Scoping Review of the Literature," *International Review of Sport and Exercise Psychology*, November 16, 2015, https://www.ncbi.nlm.nih.gov/pmc/articles/PMC4662096/.

15. National Federation of State High School Associations, "The Case for High School Activities"; "The Benefits of an Interscholastic Athletic Program"; Clark, Camiré, Wade, and Cairney, "Sport Participation and Its Association with Social and Psychological Factors Known to Predict Substance Use and Abuse among Youth."

16. Christina DesMarais, "Five Reasons Athletes Make Superior Employees," *Inc.*, November 25, 2016, www.inc.com/christina-desmarais/5-reasons-athletes-make-the-best-employees_1.html.

17. Ripley, "The Case against High School Athletics."

18. Tufte, *Crazy-Proofing High School Sports*, 90.

19. Daniel H. Bowen and Colin Hitt, "High School Sports Aren't Killing Academics," *Atlantic*, October 13, 2013, www.theatlantic.com/education/archive/2013/10/high-school-sports-arent-killing-academics/280155/.

20. Brian Gotta, "Are Sports Ruining Our High Schools?" *CoachDeck*, October 27, 2013, https://blog.coachdeck.com/2013/10/27/are-sports-ruining-our-high-schools/.

21. National Federation of State High School Associations, "High School Sports Participation Increases for 28th Straight Year, Nears 8 Million Mark," *National Federation of State High School Associations*, September 6, 2017, www.nfhs.org/articles/high-school-sports-participation-increases-for-28th-straight-year-nears-8-million-mark/.

CHAPTER 2

1. "Steve Jobs' 2005 Stanford Commencement Address," HuffPost, October 5, 2011, https://www.huffingtonpost.com/2011/10/05/steve-jobs-stanford-commencement-address_n_997301.html.

2. "Albert Bandura: Self-Efficacy for Agentic Positive Psychology," Positive Psychology Program, July 28, 2016, https://positivepsychologyprogram.com/bandura-self-efficacy/.

3. Karrah Ellis, "Self-Advocacy: Helping Student-Athletes Address Issues on Their Own," National Federation of State High School Associations, November 21, 2014, https://www.nfhs.org/articles/self-advocacy-helping-student-athletes-address-issues-on-their-own/.

4. Ellis, "Self-Advocacy."

CHAPTER 3

1. "Robert F. Kennedy, University of Capetown, Capetown, South Africa, June 6, 1966," *John F. Kennedy Presidential Library and Museum*, www.jfklibrary.org/Research/Research-Aids/Ready-Reference/RFK-Speeches/Day-of-Affirmation-Address-as-delivered.aspx.

2. Julia Zorthian, "This Is the Best Way to Recover from Failure," *Time*, September 14, 2017, http://time.com/4941487/failure-recover/; Ellie Zolfagharifard, "Failure Really *Is* Good for You: Brain Scans Reveal How We Learn from Our Mistakes Given Time," *DailyMail*, August 25, 2015, http://www.dailymail.co.uk/sciencetech/article-3210651/Failure-really-good-Brain-scans-reveal-learn-mistakes-given-time.html.

3. Noah Kagan, "Interview with Internet Marketing Party," *YouTube*, December 2, 2011, www.youtube.com/watch?v=BQWsxbXTfio&feature=youtu.be.

4. Jillian Steinhauer, "I Am the Artwork: Ai Weiwei on Film," BBC Interview of Ai Weiwei, *Paris Review*, August 2, 2012, www.theparisreview.org/blog/2012/08/02/i-am-the-artwork-ai-weiwei-on-film/.

5. W. Todd Bartko and Jacquelynne S. Eccles, "Adolescent Participation in Structured and Unstructured Activities: A Person-Oriented Analysis," *Journal of Youth and Adolescence* 32, no. (2003): 233–41.

6. John E. Tufte, *Crazy-Proofing High School Sports* (Lanham, MD: Rowman & Littlefield, 2012), 115.

7. James C. Thompson, *Developing Better Athletes, Better People: A Leader's Guide for Transporting High School and Youth Sports into a Development Zone* (Portola Valley, CA: Balance Sports, 2014), 10.

CHAPTER 4

1. "Michelangelo Buonarroti Quotes," *Goodreads*, https://www.goodreads.com/author/quotes/182763.Michelangelo_Buonarroti.

2. J. Senecal, T. M. Loughead, and G. A. Bloom, "A Season-Long Team-Building Intervention Program: Examining the Effect of Team Goal-Setting on Cohesion," *Journal of Sport and Exercise Psychology* 30, no. 2 (2008): 186–89; National Federation of State High School Associations, "The Case for High School Activities" (studies collected), *National Federation of State High School Associations*, www.nfhs.org/articles/the-case-for-high-school-activities/; "The Benefits of an Interscholastic Athletic Program" (studies collected), *Lockport City School District*, www.section6.e1b.org/cms/lib/NY19000854/Centricity/shared/ad_tool_kit/BenefitsofAthleticsBrochure.pdf; "18 Facts about Goals and Their Achievement," *Goalband*, www.goalband.co.uk/goal-achievement-facts.html.

3. Donna Merkel, "Youth Sport: Positive and Negative Impact on Young Athletes," *Open Access Journal of Sports Medicine* 4 (2013): 151–60. DOI: 10.2147/OAJSMS33556.

CHAPTER 5

1. Farrah Gray, "Comfort Is the Enemy of Achievement," *FarrahGray.com*. http://www.farrahgray.com/downloads/FREE-eBook-COMFORT-Is-The-ENEMY-Of-ACHIEVEMENT_FARRAH-GRAY.pdf.

2. Ran Zilca, "Comfort Kills," *Psychology Today*, January 27, 2011, https://www.psychologytoday.com/blog/confessions-techie/201101/comfort-kills.

3. Kathy Caprino, "Six Ways Pushing Past Your Comfort Zone Is Critical to Success," *Forbes Magazine*, May 21, 2014, www.forbes.com/sites/kathycaprino/2014/05/21/6-ways-pushing-past-your-comfort-zone-is-critical-to-success/#67e8bfab7e48.

CHAPTER 6

1. Max Nisen, "Playing High School Sports Could Give You an Advantage in the Job Market," *Quartz*, June 19, 2014, https://qz.com/223468/playing-high-school-sports-could-give-you-an-advantage-in-the-job-market/.

CHAPTER 7

1. "Alice Walker Quotes," *Goodreads*, www.goodreads.com/quotes/15083-the -most-common-way-people-give-up-their-power-is.

2. Julia Cawthra and Tina Spriggs, "Intentional Leadership Development in High School Student Athletes: A Training Program for Facilitators," Doctoral Papers and Masters Projects, Paper 28, University of Denver, 2015; Ronald E. Riggio, "What 100 Years of Research Shows about Effective Leadership," *Psychology Today*, November 20, 2009, www.psychologytoday.com/blog/cutting-edge-leadership/200911/ what-100-years-research-shows-about-effective-leadership.

3. Tim Elmore, "Is Everyone a Leader?" *Psychology Today*, February 20, 2014, www.psychologytoday.com/blog/artificial-maturity/201402/is-everyone-leader.

4. "Jim Rohn Quotes," *Goodreads*, www.goodreads.com/quotes/112552-the-chal lenge-of-leadership-is-to-be-strong-but-not.

5. Kevin M. Kniffin, Brian Wansink, and Mitsuru Shimizu, "Sports at Work: Anticipated and Persistent Correlates of Participation in High School Athletics," *Lab for Experimental Economics and Design Research, Cornell University*, 2014, http://leedr .dyson.cornell.edu/docs/SportsBiodataJLOSFinalMay7-2014.pdf.

6. Kevin M. Kniffin, "How Youth Sport Participation Leads to Career Success," *TrueSport*, August 27, 2014, http://truesportarchive.ideavise.com/youth-sport-partici pation-leads-career-success/.

CHAPTER 8

1. *Habitat for Humanity*, http://habitatmm.org/PDF's/Sponsorship/Faith%20 Brochure.pdf.

2. Bob Gardner, "High School Activities Bring Communities Together," *National Federation of State High School Associations*, August 28, 2017, www.nfhs.org/articles/ high-school-activities-bring-communities-together/.

3. "Universal Language of Sport Brings People Together, Teaches Teamwork, Tolerance, Secretary-General Says at Launch of International Year," press release of the secretary-general of the United Nations, *United Nations*, November 5, 2004, www.un.org/press/en/2004/sgsm9579.doc.htm.

4. National Federation of State High School Associations, "The Case for High School Activities" (studies collected), *National Federation of State High School Associations*, www.nfhs.org/articles/the-case-for-high-school-activities/; "The Benefits of an Interscholastic Athletic Program" (studies collected), *Lockport City School District*, http://www.section6.e1b.org/cms/lib/NY19000854/Centricity/shared/ad_tool_kit/ BenefitsofAthleticsBrochure.pdf.

5. D. R. Samek, I. J. Elkins, M. A. Keyes, W. G. Iacono, and M. McGue, "High School Sports Involvement Diminishes the Association between Childhood Conduct Disorder and Adult Antisocial Behavior," *Journal of Adolescent Health* 57, no. 1 (July 2015): 107–12. DOI: 10.1016/j.jadohealth.2015.03.009. Epub April 28, 2015.

6. "Creating Community through Sports Participation," *Journalism for Social Change*, February 26, 2016, https://chronicleofsocialchange.org/journalism-for-social-change/where-do-the-children-play.

CHAPTER 9

1. "Quote Archive," *Tiny Buddha*, https://tinybuddha.com/wisdom-quotes/you-are-very-powerful-provided-you-know-how-powerful-you-are/.

2. Kevin M. Kniffin, Brian Wansink, and Mitsuru Shimizu, "Sports at Work: Anticipated and Persistent Correlates of Participation in High School Athletics," *Lab for Experimental Economics and Design Research, Cornell University*, 2014, http://leedr.dyson.cornell.edu/docs/SportsBiodataJLOSFinalMay7-2014.pdf; National Federation of State High School Associations, "The Case for High School Activities" (studies collected), *National Federation of State High School Associations*, www.nfhs.org/articles/the-case-for-high-school-activities/; "The Benefits of an Interscholastic Athletic Program" (studies collected), *Lockport City School District*, http://www.section6.e1b.org/cms/lib/NY19000854/Centricity/shared/ad_tool_kit/Benefitsof AthleticsBrochure.pdf.

3. Kniffin, Wansink, and Shimizu, "Sports at Work"; National Federation of State High School Associations, "The Case for High School Activities"; "The Benefits of an Interscholastic Athletic Program"; Kai Sato, "The Case for High School Sports," *HuffPost*, September 27, 2013, www.huffingtonpost.com/kai-sato/high-school-sports_b_3997391.html.

4. Kniffin, Wansink, and Shimizu, "Sports at Work."

5. Sato, "The Case for High School Sports."

6. Sato, "The Case for High School Sports."

CHAPTER 10

1. "John W. Gardner Quotes," *BrainyQuote*, www.brainyquote.com/quotes/john_w_gardner_132801.

2. "Socrates Quotes," *BrainyQuote*, www.brainyquote.com/quotes/quotes/s/socrates385050.html.

3. Lewis Howl, "10 Lessons for Entrepreneurs from Coach John Wooden," *Forbes Business*, October 19, 2012, www.forbes.com/sites/lewishowes/2012/10/19/10-lessons-for-entrepreneurs-from-coach-john-wooden/#731e847916d5.

CHAPTER 11

1. *Pinterest*, www.pinterest.com/pin/271693789993112630/.

2. Colette Lange, "Sports Success Stories, Character, and Personal Development," *University of Houston*, 2002, www.uh.edu/honors/Programs-Minors/honors-and

-the-schools/houston-teachers-institute/curriculum-units/pdfs/2002/sports-autobio
graphies/lange-02-sports.pdf, 4.

3. "Lao Tzu Quotes," *BrainyQuote*, www.brainyquote.com/quotes/quotes/l/
laotzu130742.html.

4. *Wikipedia*, https://en.wikipedia.org/wiki/A_journey_of_a_thousand_miles_be
gins_with_a_single_step.

CHAPTER 12

1. "Rollo May Quotes," *BrainyQuote*, www.brainyquote.com/quotes/rollo_may
_389414.

2. Nicholas Bragg, "Effective Communication in Sports," *Livestrong.com*, September 17, 2011, www.livestrong.com/article/220761-effective-communication-in
-sports/.

3. Kostya Kennedy, *Lasting Impact: One Team, One Season. What Happens When
Our Sons Play Football* (Tampa, FL: Liberty Street, 2016), 53.

CHAPTER 13

1. *PassItOn.com*, www.passiton.com/inspirational-quotes/6529-its-not-hard-to
-make-decisions-when-you-know.

2. Joe Ehrmann, *InSideOut Coaching: How Sports Can Transform Lives* (New York:
Simon & Schuster, 2011), 159.

CHAPTER 14

1. "The Most Important Trait in a Struggle," *Ziglar*, November 23, 2009, https://
tziglar.wordpress.com/tag/john-maxwell/.

2. Annalisa Merelli, "The Habit That Gets in the Way of Success and How
Olympic Athletes Avoid It," *Quartz*, August 11, 2016, https://qz.com/755046/how
-olympic-athletes-stay-motivated/.

CHAPTER 15

1. "Albert Einstein," *Today in Science History*, https://todayinsci.com/E/Einstein
_Albert/EinsteinAlbert-ProblemQuote800px.htm.

2. Neela Dongrel and R. C. Pate. "Development of Problem-Solving Skill of Adolescents through Teaching of Science for Sustainable Development," *IOSR Journal of*

Humanities and Social Science 20, no. 7, ver. III (July 2015): 46–52, www.iosrjournals
.org/iosr-jhss/papers/Vol20-issue7/Version-3/H020734652.pdf.

3. Quinn Phillips, "Study Shows That Girls in Sports Develop Conflict-Resolution Skills," *Phys.org*, May 12, 2009, https://phys.org/news/2009-05-girls-sports-conflict-resolution-skills.html.

CHAPTER 16

1. "Joseph LeConte Quotes," *Goodreads*, www.goodreads.com/quotes/659460
-the-essential-thing-is-not-knowledge-but-character/.

2. Richard V. Reeves, Kimberly Howard, and Joanna Venator, "The Character Factor: Measures and Impact of Drive and Prudence," *Center on Children and Families, Brookings Institution*, October 22, 2014, www.brookings.edu/wp-content/
uploads/2016/06/The-Character-Factor.pdf; Evie Blad, "For Success in Life, Character Matters as Much as Academic Skill, Study Says," *Education Week*, October 22, 2014, http://blogs.edweek.org/edweek/rulesforengagement/2014/10/for_success_in
_life_character_matters_as_much_as_academic_skill_study_says.html.

3. James C. Thompson, *Developing Better Athletes, Better People: A Leader's Guide for Transporting High School and Youth Sports into a Development Zone* (Portola Valley, CA: Balance Sports, 2014), 3.

4. Thompson, *Developing Better Athletes, Better People*, 5.

5. Joe Ehrmann, *InSideOut Coaching: How Sports Can Transform Lives* (New York: Simon & Schuster, 2011), 121, 218.

6. James C. Thompson, *Positive Coaching: Building Character and Self-Esteem through Sports* (Portola Valley, CA: Warde, 1995), 123.

CHAPTER 17

1. "John Wooden Quotes," *Life Sayings and Quotes*, www.lifesayingsquotes.com/
quote/being-role-model-powerful-form-199/.

2. Marilyn Price-Mitchell, "How Role Models Influence Youth Strategies for Success," *Roots of Action*, www.rootsofaction.com/role-models-youth-strategies
-success/; Susan Krauss Whitbourne, "We All Need Role Models to Motivate and Inspire Us," *Psychology Today*, November 19, 2013, www.psychologytoday.com/blog/
fulfillment-any-age/201311/we-all-need-role-models-motivate-and-inspire-us.

3. Cheechee Lin, "A Leader's Most Powerful Ally Is His or Her Own Example," *UCLA Anderson Blog*, October 5, 2015, http://blogs.anderson.ucla.edu/
anderson/2015/10/a-leaders-most-powerful-ally-is-his-or-her-own-example-coach
-john-wooden.html.

4. Gordon A. Bloom, Natalie Durand-Bush, Robert J. Schinke, and John H. Salmela, "The Importance of Mentoring in the Development of Coaches and Athletes," *Sport Psychol*, 1998, http://sportpsych.mcgill.ca/pdf/publications/mentoring.pdf.

5. "Research on Big Brothers Big Sisters," *Big Brothers Big Sisters of America*, www.bbbs.org/research/.

6. "Student Athletes in Touch: About Us," *Student Athletes in Touch*, http://studentathletesintouch.com/about_us.html.

CHAPTER 18

1. "Buddha Quotes," *BrainyQuote*, www.brainyquote.com/quotes/buddha_387356.

2. "NIH Study Finds Leisure-Time Physical Activity Extends Life Expectancy as Much as 4.5 Years," *National Cancer Institute*, November 6, 2012, www.cancer.gov/news-events/press-releases/2012/PhysicalActivityLifeExpectancy; Michael Brent, "The Importance of Physical Fitness as a Teenager," *Livestrong.com*, 2017, www.livestrong.com/article/541372-the-importance-of-physical-fitness-as-a-teenager/; Arlene Semeco, "The Top 10 Benefits of Regular Exercise," *Healthline*, 2017, www.healthline.com/nutrition/10-benefits-of-exercise#section11; Mayo Staff Clinic, "Exercise: Seven Benefits of Regular Physical Activity," *Mayo Clinic*, 2016, www.mayoclinic.org/healthy-lifestyle/fitness/in-depth/exercise/art-20048389?pg=2.

3. Harold Kohl and Heather Cook, with the Institute of Medicine, "Educating the Student Body: Taking Physical Activity and Physical Education to School" (Washington, DC: National Academies Press, 2013), http://labs.kch.illinois.edu/Research/Labs/neurocognitive-kinesiology/files/Articles/Full%20Report_EducatingTheStudentBody.pdf.

4. Russell R. Pate, Stewart G. Trost, Sarah Levin, and Marsha Dowda, "Sports Participation and Health-Related Behaviors among U.S. Youth," *Archives of Pediatrics and Adolescent Medicine* 154, no. 9 (September 2000): 904–11. DOI: 10.1001/archpedi.154.9.904.

5. Kirsten Weir, "The Exercise Effect," *American Psychological Association*, December 2011, www.apa.org/monitor/2011/12/exercise.aspx; Donna Merkel, "Youth Sport: Positive and Negative Impact on Young Athletes," *Open Access Journal of Sports Medicine* 4 (2013): 151–60. DOI: 10.2147/OAJSMS33556.

6. "What Is the Mind–Body Connection?" *University of Minnesota*, 2016, www.takingcharge.csh.umn.edu/what-is-the-mind-body-connection.

7. Mel Schwartz, "Beyond the Mind–Body Connection," *Psychology Today*, January 23, 2010, www.psychologytoday.com/blog/shift-mind/201001/beyond-the-mind-body-connection.

8. Thich Nhat Hanh, *How to Love* (Berkeley, CA: Parallax Press, 2015), 31.

9. Kyle Hunt, "Exercise and the MindBody Connection," *Hunt Fitness*, April 10, 2012, www.kylehuntfitness.com/exercise-and-the-mind-body-connection/.

10. Sophia Breene, "13 Mental Health Benefits of Exercise," *HuffPost*, March 27, 2013, www.huffingtonpost.com/2013/03/27/mental-health-benefits-exercise_n_2956099.html.

11. "Fit after 50: Staying Flexible with Yoga," *KareenAbdulJabbar.com*, https://kareemabduljabbar.com/fit-after-50-staying-flexible-with-yoga/.

12. Michael Popke, "High School Sports Teams Stretch Out with Yoga," *Athletic Business*, February 2012, www.athleticbusiness.com/High-School/high-school -sports-teams-stretch-out-with-yoga.html.

13. "Yoga Shows Psychological Benefits for High School Students," *Science Daily*, April 4, 2012, www.sciencedaily.com/releases/2012/04/120404101824.htm.

14. Hunt, "Exercise and the MindBody Connection."

CHAPTER 19

1. "Coilin Powell Quotes," *BrainyQuote*, www.brainyquote.com/quotes/colin _powell_163071.

2. James Clear, "How Positive Thinking Builds Your Skills, Boosts Your Health, and Improves Your Work," *Behavioral Psychology*, 2018, https://jamesclear.com/posi tive-thinking; Karen Feldscher, "How Positive Thinking Works," *Harvard Gazette*, December 7, 2016, https://news.harvard.edu/gazette/story/2016/12/optistic-women -live-longer-are-healthier/; Jane Brody, "A Positive Outlook May Be Good for Your Health," *New York Times*, March 27, 2017, www.nytimes.com/2017/03/27/well/live/ positive-thinking-may-improve-health-and-extend-life.html; "The Power of Positive Thinking," *John Hopkins Medicine*, www.hopkinsmedicine.org/health/healthy_aging/ healthy_mind/the-power-of-positive-thinking.

3. Brody, "A Positive Outlook May Be Good for Your Health."

4. Feldscher, "How Positive Thinking Works."

5. Tom Vander Ark, "School Culture and Relationships Thrive with a 5:1 Positivity Ratio," *Education Week*, January 23, 2017, http://blogs.edweek.org/edweek/ on_innovation/2017/01/school_culture_and_relationships_thrive_with_a_51_posi tivity_ratio.html.

6. James C. Thompson, *Positive Coaching: Building Character and Self-Esteem through Sports* (Portola Valley, CA: Warde, 1995), 42.

7. Clear, "How Positive Thinking Builds Your Skills."

8. Thompson, *Positive Coaching*, 111.

CONCLUSION

1. John Dewey, "My Pedagogic Creed," *School Journal* 54 (January 1897): 78.

Suggested Reading

Adelman, C. *Light and Shadows on College Athletes: College Transcripts and Labor Market History*. Research Report, Office of Educational Research and Improvement. Washington, DC: U.S. Department of Education, 1990.

Afremow, Jim. *The Champion's Mind: How Great Athletes Think, Train, and Thrive*. New York: Rodale, 2015.

Allen, Phog. *Coach Phog Allen's Sports Stories*. Lawrence, KS: Allen Press, 1947.

Barron, J. M., B. T. Ewing, and G. R. Waddell. "The Effects of High School Athletic Participation on Education and Labor Market Outcomes." *Review of Economics and Statistics* 82 (2000): 409–21.

Bilas, Jay. *Toughness: Developing True Strength on and off the Court*. New York: Penguin, 2014.

Biles, Simone. *Courage to Soar: A Body in Motion, a Life in Balance*. Grand Rapids, MI: Zondervan, 2016.

Blais, Madeline. *In These Girls, Hope Is a Muscle*. New York: Warner Books, 1995.

Block, Peter. *Community: The Structure of Belonging*. San Francisco, CA: Berrett-Koehler, 2009.

Bloom, B. S., ed. *Developing Talent in Young People*. New York: Ballantine, 1985.

Bos, Candace S., Donald D. Deshler, Jean B. Schumaker, and Anthony K. Van Reusen. *The Self-Advocacy Strategy for Enhancing Student Motivation and Self-Determination (an Education and Transition Planning Process)*. Lawrence, KS: Edge Enterprises, 2007.

Branden, Nathaniel. *The Six Pillars of Self-Esteem: The Definitive Work on Self-Esteem by the Leading Pioneer in the Field*. New York: Bantam, 1995.

Brooks, David. *The Road to Character*. New York: Random House, 2015.

Brounstein, Marty. *Coaching and Mentoring for Dummies*. Foster City, CA: IDG Books Worldwide, 2000.

Burson, Jim. *The Golden Whistle, Going Beyond: The Journey to Coaching Success*. Tucson, AZ: Jetlaunch Premium Publishing, 2014.

Bush, A. J., C. A. Martin, and P. W. Clark. "The Effect of Role Model Influence on Adolescents' Materialism and Marketplace Knowledge." *Journal of Marketing Theory and Practice* 9, no. 4 (2001): 27–36.

Caouya, John. *Real Men Do Yoga: 21 Star Athletes Reveal Their Secrets of Strength, Flexibility, and Peak Performance.* Deerfield Beach, FL: Health Communications, 2003.

Coyle, Daniel. *The Talent Code: Greatness Isn't Born. It's Grown. Here's How.* New York, New York: Bantam Dell.

Danois, Alejandro. *The Boys of Dunbar: A Story of Love, Hope, and Basketball.* New York: Simon & Schuster, 2016.

Day, D. V., S. Gordon, and C. Fink. "The Sporting Life: Exploring Organizations through the Lens of Sport." *Academy of Management Annals* 6 (2012): 1–37.

Donnelly, Darrin. *Old School Grit: Times May Change, but the Rules of Success Never Do.* Sports for the Soul, vol. 2. Lenexa, KS: Shamrock New Media, 2016.

———. *Relentless Optimism: How a Commitment to Positive Thinking Changes Everything.* Sports for the Soul, vol. 3. Lenexa, KS: Shamrock New Media, 2017.

———. *Think Like a Warrior: The Five Inner Beliefs That Make You Unstoppable.* Sports for the Soul, vol. 1. Lenexa, KS: Shamrock New Media, 2016.

Duhigg, Charles. *The Power of HABIT: Why We Do What We Do in Life and Business.* New York: Random House, 2012.

Dungy, Tony, and Nathan Whitaker. *Quiet Strength: The Principles, Practices, and Priorities of a Winning Life.* Carol Stream, IL: Tyndale House, 2008.

Dweck, Carol S. *Mindset, the New Psychology of Success: How We Can Learn to Fulfill Our Potential.* New York: Random House, 2006.

Ehrmann, Joe. *InSideOut Coaching: How Sports Can Transform Lives.* New York: Simon & Schuster, 2011.

Ewing, B. T. "The Labor Market Effects of High School Athletic Participation: Evidence from Wage and Fringe Benefit Differentials." *Journal of Sports Economics* 8 (2007): 255–65.

Finch, Jennie, and Ann Killion. *Throw Like a Girl: How to Dream Big and Believe in Yourself.* Chicago: Triumph, 2011.

Fisher, R., and W. Ury. *Getting to Yes.* New York: Penguin, 1991.

Girard, K., and S. J. Koch. *Conflict Resolution in the Schools: A Manual for Educators.* San Francisco, CA: Jossey-Bass, 1996.

Goldsmith, Marshall, Laurence S. Lyons, and Sarah McArthur. *Coaching for Leadership: Writings on Leadership from the World's Greatest Coaches.* San Francisco, CA: John Wiley & Sons, 2015.

Goleman, Daniel. *Emotional Intelligence: Why It Can Matter More Than IQ.* New York: Bantam, 1995.

Gonzalez, D. C., and Alice McVeigh. *The Art of Mental Training: A Guide to Performance Excellence.* CreateSpace Independent Publishing, 2013.

Gordon, Jon, and Mike Smith. *You Win in the Locker Room First: The 7 C's to Build a Winning Team in Business, Sports, and Life.* Hoboken, NJ: John Wiley & Sons, 2015.

Gross, B., and G. Zimmerman. *Mediating Interpersonal Conflict.* North Manchester, IN: Education for Conflict Resolution, 1997.

Grove, Tim S., and Shari Wenk. *Relentless: From Good to Great to Unstoppable.* New York: Relentless Publishing, 2014.

Hammond, John S., Ralph S. Keeney, and Howard Raiffa. *Smart Choices: A Practical Guide to Making Better Decisions.* Boston: Harvard Business Review Press, 2015.

Harvey, Thomas, and Bonita Drolet. *Building Teams, Building People*, 2nd ed. Lanham, MD: Rowman & Littlefield Education, 2004.

Jackson, Phil, and Hugh Delehanty. *Eleven Rings: The Soul of Success.* New York: Penguin, 2014.

———. *Sacred Hoops: Spiritual Lessons of a Hardwood Warrior.* New York: Hyperion, 1995.

Jackson, S. A., and M. Csikszentmihalyi. *Flow in Sports.* Champaign, IL: Human Kinetics, 1999.

Kay, Katie, and Claire Shipman. *The Confidence Code: The Science and Art of Self-Assurance—What Women Should Know.* New York: HarperCollins, 2014.

Kennedy, Kostya. *Lasting Impact: One Team, One Season. What Happens When Our Sons Play Football.* Tampa, FL: Liberty Street, 2016.

Krzyzewski, Mike, and Jamie K. Spatola. *Beyond Basketball: Coach K's Keywords for Success.* New York: Warner Business Books, 2007.

Krzyzewski, Mike, with Donald T. Phillips. *Leading with the Heart: Coach K's Successful Strategies for Basketball, Business, and Life.* New York: Warner Business Books, 2001.

Lahey, Jessica. *The Gift of Failure: How the Best Parents Learn to Let Go So Their Children Can Succeed.* New York: Harper, 2016.

Leal, Bento C., III. *Four Essential Keys to Effective Communication in Love, Life, Work—Anywhere! Including the "12-Day Communication Challenge!"* CreateSpace Independent Publishing, 2017.

Lyubomirsky, S. *The How of Happiness: A New Approach to Getting the Life You Want*[e-book]. New York: Penguin, 2008.

Martin, Cory. *Yoga for Beginners: Simple Yoga Poses to Calm Your Mind and Strengthen Your Body.* Berkeley, CA: Rockridge Press, 2015.

Martin, N. J. "Keeping It Fun in Youth Sport: What Coaches Should Know and Do." *Strategies* 27, no. 5 (2014): 27–32.

Maxwell, John C. *The 17 Indisputable Laws of Teamwork: Embrace Them and Empower Your Team.* Nashville, TN: Thomas Nelson, 2013.

Maxwell, John C., and Steven R. Covey. *The 21 Irrefutable Laws of Leadership: Follow Them and People Will Follow You.* Nashville, TN: Thomas Nelson, 2007. Originally printed in 1998.

McGregor, Jena. "The Relentless Positivity of Chicago Cubs Manager Joe Madden." *Washington Post*, October 26, 2016, www.washingtonpost.com/news/on-leadership/wp/2016/10/26/the-relentless-positivity-of-chicago-cubs-manager-joe-maddon/?utm_term=.babd2f842d5a.Miller, Rory. *Conflict Communication (ConCom): A New Paradigm in Conscious Communication.* Wolfeboro, NH: YMAA Publications Center, 2015.

Molinsky, Andy. *Reach: A New Strategy to Help You Step Outside Your Comfort Zone, Rise to the Challenge, and Build Confidence.* New York: Penguin/Random House, 2017.

Mumford, George. *The Mindful Athlete: Secrets to Pure Performance*. Berkeley, CA: Parallax, 2016.

Pasricha, Neil. *The Book of Awesome*. New York: Putnam, 2010.

Pierson, Carl J. *The Politics of Coaching, A Survival Guide to Keep Coaches from Getting Burned*. CreateSpace Independent Publishing, 2011.

Price, S. L. *Playing through the Whistle: Steel, Football, and an American Town*. New York: Grove Press, 2016.

Pruter, Robert. *The Rise of American High School Sports and the Search for Control: 1880–1930*. Syracuse, NY: Syracuse University Press, 2013.

Rountree, Sage. *The Athlete's Pocket Guide to Yoga: 50 Routines for Flexibility, Balance, and Focus* [spiral-bound]. Boulder, CO: Velo Press, 2009.

Simpson, Michael K. *Unlocking Potential: Seven Coaching Skills That Transform Individuals, Teams, and Organizations*. Grand Haven, MI: Grand Harbor Press, 2014.

Stainer, Michael Bungay. *The Coaching Habit: Say Less, Ask More, and Change the Way You Lead Forever*. Toronto, Ontario, Canada: Box of Crayons Press, 2016.

Stoltzfus, Tony. *Coaching Questions: A Coach's Guide to Powerful Asking Skills*. Virginia Beach, VA: Tony Stoltzfus, 2008.

Summit, Pat Head. *Raise the Roof: The Inspiring Inside Story of the Tennessee Lady Vols' Historic 1997–1998 Three-Peat Season*. New York: Random House, 1998.

———. *Reach for the Summit: The Definite Dozen System for Succeeding at Whatever You*. New York: Random House, 1998.

Swanson, J. A., K. B. Kowalski, H. J. Gettman, and J. Lee. "Leadership Characteristics and Title IX: A Possible Mechanism for the Impact of Sports Participation on Work Outcomes." *International Leadership Journal* 4 (2012): 40–61.

Taylor, Erin. *Hit Reset: Revolutionary Yoga for Athletes*. Boulder, CO: Velo Press, 2016.

Thompson, James C. *Developing Better Athletes, Better People: A Leader's Guide for Transporting High School and Youth Sports into a Development Zone*. Portola Valley, CA: Balance Sports, 2014.

———. *Positive Coaching: Building Character and Self-Esteem through Sports*. Portola Valley, CA: Warde, 1995.

———. *The Power of Double-Goal Coaching: Developing Winners in Sports and Life*. Portola Valley, CA: Balance Sports, 2010.

Toropov, B. *The Art and Skill of Dealing with People*. Paramus, NJ: Prentice Hall, 1997.

Tracy, Brian. *Goals! How to Get Everything You Want—Faster Than You Ever Thought Possible*. San Francisco, CA: Berrett-Koehler, 2010.

Trieste, Chris. *14 Great Coaches: Learn Their Lessons, Improve Your Coaching, Have a Lasting Impact*. CreateSpace Independent Publishing, 2017.

Tufte, John E. *Crazy-Proofing High School Sports*. Lanham, MD: Rowman & Littlefield, 2012.

Vella, S., L. Oades, and T. Crowe. "The Role of the Coach in Facilitating Positive Youth Development: Moving from Theory to Practice." *Journal of Applied Sports Psychology* 23, no. 1 (2011): 33–48.

Vigue, Sean. *Power Yoga for Athletes: More Than 100 Poses and Flows to Improve Performance in Any Sport.* Beverly, MA: Fair Winds Press, 2015.

Walsh, Bill, with Steve Jamison and Craig Walsh. *The Score Takes Care of Itself: My Philosophy of Leadership.* New York: Penguin, 2010.

Wooden, John, and Jay Carty. *Coach Wooden's Pyramid of Success Playbook.* Grand Rapids, MI: Revel, 2005.

Wooden, John, and Steve Jamison. *Wooden on Leadership: How to Create a Winning Organization.* New York: McGraw-Hill, 2005.

Wooden, John, with Steve Jamison. *Wooden: A Lifetime of Observations and Reflections on and off the Court.* New York: McGraw-Hill, 1997.

Wooden, John, and Jack Tobin. *They Call Me Coach.* New York: McGraw-Hill, 1998.

Index

About the Author

Michael Coffino was a litigation attorney for 36 years and, in parallel with his legal career, spent 24 years as a basketball coach, primarily at the high school level. He is now a full-time writer. He is author of *Odds-On Basketball Coaching: Crafting High-Percentage Strategies for Game Situations* and coauthor of a memoir entitled *Play It Forward: From Gymboree to the Yoga Mat and Beyond*. Coffino recently finished writing a memoir for another client and has completed a comprehensive handbook for the beginner high school basketball head coach, and currently is working on his first work of fiction. He was born in the Bronx and grew up in its Highbridge section. He plays guitar and holds a black belt in karate. Coffino has two adult sons, both elementary school teachers and high school basketball coaches, and lives in Tiburon, California.